The

WISDOM

of

COMPASSION

www.**transworldbooks**.co.uk

The

WISDOM

of

COMPASSION

*Stories of Remarkable Encounters
and Timeless Insights*

HIS HOLINESS
THE DALAI LAMA
and Victor Chan

BANTAM PRESS

LONDON · TORONTO · SYDNEY · AUCKLAND · JOHANNESBURG

TRANSWORLD PUBLISHERS
61–63 Uxbridge Road, London W5 5SA
A Random House Group Company
www.transworldbooks.co.uk

First Published in the United States
in 2012 by Riverhead Books,
the Penguin Group

First published in Great Britain
in 2012 by Bantam Press
an imprint of Transworld Publishers

A CIP catalogue record for this book
is available from the British Library.

ISBN 9780593071823

Addresses for Random House Group Ltd companies outside the UK
can be found at: www.randomhouse.co.uk
The Random House Group Ltd Reg. No. 954009

The Random House Group Limited supports the Forest Stewardship Council (FSC®), the
leading international forest-certification organization. Our books carrying the FSC label
are printed on FSC®-certified paper. FSC is the only forest-certification scheme endorsed by
the leading environmental organizations, including Greenpeace. Our paper procurement
policy can be found at www.randomhouse.co.uk/environment.

Typeset in Spectrum MT
Printed and bound in Great Britain by
CPI Group(UK) Ltd, Croydon, CRO 4YY

2 4 6 8 10 9 7 5 3

Susanne, Lina, and Kira

—V.C.

CONTENTS

III. COMPASSION IN ACTION

Preface

WHAT THE DALAI LAMA KNOWS FOR SURE

Every morning for more than half a century, the Dalai Lama has woken up at three-thirty a.m. After a quick shower (he is not one to use excess water by taking a bath), he settles into a well-ordered routine of prayers and meditation that lasts for five hours. He uses some of this time to "shape his motivation" for the rest of the day. He is grateful that he is alive, and he sees each moment as a precious opportunity to open his heart and to do everything within his power to be of service to others. And he reminds himself that he will hold only kind thoughts to all.

For much of the morning, the Dalai Lama meditates on altruistic love and compassion, "to generate a sense of caring," he says, "to foster genuine concern for others' difficulties and pain, and to develop close, warmhearted feelings for others. Not only for my family and close friends, but also for everyone. Enemies, too." He internalizes the desire that everyone be truly happy and be free of suffering. By means of this process, through more than a hundred thousand hours of disciplined practice, the Dalai Lama has embedded compassion into every fiber of his being— like oil soaking a cloth. And, by meditating on compassion regularly, he has made significant improvements to his own well-being.

The Dalai Lama believes that our purpose in life is to be happy. He was thirty-two when, after years of perseverance, he arrived at a profound understanding of compassion. "Since that time, my mind became familiar with the feeling of compassion, that feeling very strong. Often when I reflect on the meaning and benefits of altruistic mind, tears come." The Dalai Lama has arrived at a key insight: that by cultivating compassion, we achieve ultimate happiness for ourselves. He calls this "wise selfish."

"Helping others does not mean we do this at our own expense," he says. "Buddhas and other enlightened beings are very wise. Throughout their lives they want only one thing: to achieve ultimate happiness. How to do this? Be altruistic, cultivate compassion. When they care for others, they themselves are the first to benefit—they are the first to get maximum happiness. They know that the best way to lead happy life is to help others. That is real wisdom."

The latest research in neuroscience shows that when compassion suffuses our minds, when we care keenly for the welfare of others, the left prefrontal cortex of our brain becomes noticeably more active. This is a clear sign that positive emotions— well-being, enthusiasm, contentment—are coursing through

Preface

us. This comes as no surprise to the Dalai Lama. He has said all along that if you want others to be happy, practice compassion; if you want to be happy, practice compassion.

This is a book about the wisdom of compassion, about how concern for others inexorably leads us to deep-rooted well-being. It is a behind-the-curtain look at the inimitable way that the Dalai Lama embodies and exercises compassion. This is the Dalai Lama in context—live, unscripted, and at his most charismatic. Through stories of his interactions with diverse people on four continents, we are gently instructed in the cultivation of happiness.

The three sections of the book reflect the idea of compassion in thought ("Overcoming Adversity"), speech ("Educating the Heart"), and action ("Compassion in Action").

In "Overcoming Adversity," the Dalai Lama speaks to sick children, ex-prisoners, and victims of the Northern Ireland conflict. He listens to their heartbreaking stories and explains that widening our perspective can help us deal with challenges.

The practice of compassion goes beyond thinking caring thoughts. The Dalai Lama encourages us to learn holistically, to incorporate the values of empathy and altruism, in addition to achieving academic excellence, in our classrooms. In "Educating the Heart," he converses with high school students and shares his thoughts on how we can nurture the seed of compassion throughout our lives. He suggests that the causes of most of our problems are not external but are in our own minds. Anger, attachment, and ignorance are the real sources of our unhappiness.

Preface

If we are compassionate, it is natural that we should want to actively help others. In the "Compassion in Action" section, the Dalai Lama meets leading social entrepreneurs and activists who have made a significant difference in the lives of underprivileged people in India and Africa. He is impressed with their innovative and highly effective approaches and shares his own personal stories of compassionate giving.

It is my hope that these stories will make a small contribution to the question "Who is the Dalai Lama?" And that the insights that the stories provide, whether through the Dalai Lama's words or through the singular way in which he relates to people, will offer simple clues that can help us live our lives more fully.

Victor Chan

KIRA'S PROSTRATIONS

*Genuine compassion is based not on our own projections and
expectations but rather on the rights of the other: irrespective
of whether another person is a close friend or an enemy, as
long as that person wishes for peace and happiness and wishes
to overcome suffering, then on that basis we develop a genuine
concern for his or her problems. If you want others to be happy,
practice compassion. If you want to be happy, practice
compassion.*

—*His Holiness the Dalai Lama*

The Dalai Lama's face brightened when he saw the man
with tinted glasses approach. He immediately stood up,
walked to the edge of the small stage, and extended a
hand toward Richard Moore. "Here, here, one small step here.
Careful, careful," he said as he grabbed the man's right hand,
guided him up the low platform and to a chair.

"Comfortable?" he asked.

"Very comfortable," Moore said. The Irishman was dressed

simply in a black windbreaker and slacks. He was in his late forties, and his light brown hair was thinning.

The Dalai Lama cleared his throat, gave his shaved head a good scratch, and said to the forty or so humanitarians seated in rows before him in a small conference room in a hotel in Delhi, "Since we met, I learned about Richard's story. A British soldier shot him when he was ten years old. With rubber bullet, hit here——" The Tibetan leader pointed at his own right eye. "And instantly his eyes lost. He fainted. When he woke up, he already in hospital. His first feeling: Now no longer I can see my mother's face." The Dalai Lama placed his hand over his heart and said, "Very touching."

As one of the organizers of the Dalai Lama's 2011 dialogue with prominent social activists from four continents, I had thought it important that he spend some time onstage with Richard Moore. I had witnessed the special chemistry between them, which had developed during their first meeting in 2000 in Derry, Northern Ireland. At that time, the Dalai Lama had been curious to know how long it took for Moore to get over the traumatic loss of his eyesight. "Overnight. I learned to see life in a different way," the Irishman had told him. Then the Dalai Lama had asked how he felt about the man who shot him. Moore had replied without any hesitation, "From the beginning I felt no ill will toward the soldier."

"No anger. So wonderful," the Dalai Lama told the group in Delhi, admiration in his voice. "Without much study or much practice, I think Richard utilize basic human good nature and human wisdom. His eyesight lost. Anger never bring back. Hatred never bring back. Instead of that, more compassion, with spirit of forgiveness. His mental state much happier. He is my hero."

I have known the Dalai Lama for four decades. I have traveled extensively with him, attended many of his lectures and dialogues. I have seen him in the company of students, rock stars, philanthropists, and beggars. Over the years, I have become familiar with—and come to love—the idiosyncratic way he uses the English language to illustrate his points and the way he interacts with people on an intimate level. I am not surprised that he singled out and befriended Richard Moore, someone who suffered a devastating loss in his youth.

However, I have never heard the Dalai Lama call anyone else his hero.

I met the Dalai Lama for the first time in 1972. The meeting came about because of an unexpected incident: I had been kidnapped, earlier that year, in Kabul, Afghanistan.

After finishing college in Canada, I had bought a used VW camper in Utrecht, painted it a psychedelic purple, and driven it overland to Afghanistan. In a backpacker hotel in Kabul, I met Cheryl Crosby, a thirtysomething New Yorker. We were drinking tea in a chai shop with Rita, a young German traveler, when three Afghan men abducted us at gunpoint. In the dead of winter and in pitch darkness, we were driven to Paghman, the summer resort of the Afghan kings high up in the Hindu Kush. By a stroke of good luck, we managed to escape three days later, when, as the kidnappers were driving us out of the small village, their beat-up Datsun flipped on the snowy switchbacks. We scrambled out of the car, ran down the mountain, and managed to hitch a ride back to Kabul in a truck.

After this harrowing experience, Cheryl and I decided to travel together to India. It turned out that she had a letter of introduction to the Dalai Lama through her connections in New York. It was during the festivities of Holi in March 1972 (we got out of the bus in Dharamsala and were promptly pelted with little balloons filled with colored water) that we were granted an audience in the Tibetan leader's home.

Several things about that encounter still stand out for me. I vividly remember that the Dalai Lama had a hard time suppressing his giggles whenever he looked my way. My hair was down to the small of my back and unkempt; I was dressed all in black: embroidered shirt, threadbare velvet pants, and an ankle-length flowing Moroccan cape. The Dalai Lama's English was poor at the time and his secretary translated the exchange between him and Cheryl. I only managed to blurt out one question: "Do you hate the Chinese?" He straightened in his chair and spoke forcefully in English for the first time, "No. I do not hate the Chinese." Then his secretary translated, "His Holiness considers the Chinese his brothers and sisters."

∾

The second time I met the Dalai Lama was in London, twenty-two years later, in 1994. I presented him with a copy of the newly published *Tibet Handbook*, a 1,100-page guide to the pilgrimage places of Tibet, which I had spent ten years researching and writing.

❧

I met the Tibetan leader for the third time in 1999, in Indiana.

He walked alone onto the stage in the Indianapolis stadium. He was bent low, almost double, as he walked to the center. One palm was raised face level and vertical to the floor in a traditional Buddhist greeting. He bowed to the audience, first left, then right, then straight ahead. Forty-five hundred people applauded loudly. He would give a talk here before moving on to Bloomington to preside over the Kalachakra Empowerment, an eleven-day Buddhist ritual to enhance world peace.

The Dalai Lama was welcomed by Indianapolis's mayor and the state's governor. He presented them both with white silk scarves, the traditional Tibetan greeting, carefully draping them around their necks. Then he walked to the podium. Just as he was about to step behind the microphone, he hesitated and gestured to someone in the wings. His private secretary, Tenzin Geyche Tethong, a middle-aged man in a gray Tibetan robe, came out and handed him another white scarf. The Dalai Lama took it and walked to the edge of the stage. He bent down until his face was almost level with his brown oxfords. From there, he draped the scarf around the sign-language interpreter standing below. As he held the face of the surprised woman in his hands, he beamed at her. Then he straightened up and walked back to the podium.

Unexpectedly, I teared up.

I was surprised at my reaction. For most of my life, under the influence of my Chinese culture and upbringing, I have had my emotions under tight control. I had a hard time making sense of what had happened now: where the tears came from, why they flowed so unexpectedly.

Toward the end of the ceremony in Bloomington, I got word that the Dalai Lama would see my family and me. At the appointed time, Tenzin Taklha, a nephew of the Dalai Lama's, ushered us into the audience room. The Dalai Lama stood near the door, waiting.

I was determined to follow protocol by prostrating myself before the Dalai Lama—the requisite three full-length, body-stretched-out-on-the-floor prostrations. As I self-consciously went through the unfamiliar ritual, my wife, Susanne, did the same.

When I stood up, I noticed that the Dalai Lama was chuckling to himself. Next to my feet, I saw that Kira, my then three-year-old daughter, was lying flat on the floor, her arms stretched all the way out in front of her. She unhurriedly stood up, put her palms together, and brought them in sequence to her forehead, throat, and heart. Then she was down on the floor again, finishing her third and last prostration. Kira had never done this before, but I could see she had the ritual down pat. She completed her prostrations as precisely, as gracefully, as any experienced monk. I stole a glance at Susanne. She had tears in her eyes. My elder daughter, six-year-old Lina, stood awkwardly with her eyes fixed on the floor. She seemed embarrassed by her family's antics.

The meeting in Bloomington was another watershed moment in my life. It was there that the Dalai Lama agreed to coauthor a book, *The Wisdom of Forgiveness*, with me. I had made the pitch, and to my surprise, he readily agreed.

Since then, for more than a decade, I have been fortunate to spend many hours interviewing the Dalai Lama in his home and traveling with him throughout North America, Europe, Asia, and even the Arctic. An added bonus has been the opportunity to meet many of the remarkable men and women who seek out the Dalai Lama and to be present at life-affirming conversations and dialogues.

❧

Over the years I have often wondered about the myriad pathways through which the Dalai Lama touches people, about the impact he has on so many throughout the world. Take the curious moment in Indianapolis. My family and I had driven to the event from our home in Vancouver, Canada, in a 1982 Westfalia camper (yes, yet another VW camper). It had been a long and less than pleasant trip: car troubles, the sweltering heat of the Midwest, long hours at the wheel. We arrived in the city and I picked up a complimentary ticket for the Dalai Lama's address. I was late for the event, bone-tired, and had to settle for a seat high up in the stadium. The Dalai Lama was a long way off; I could barely make out his features. And yet, without his uttering a word, something about his manner, something about his presence, had a powerful impact on me.

The Dalai Lama affects people in different ways. Many go to see him because they are curious, drawn to him because he is a global celebrity. Or they expect that his teachings can help them lead a more fulfilling life.

Some people react to the Dalai Lama in less favorable ways. In a washroom in a synagogue on Wilshire Boulevard in Los Angeles, I overheard two businessmen exchanging notes about a talk given by the Dalai Lama that they had just heard. They were dismissive. They thought that the talk was simplistic; it didn't meet their expectations. On another occasion, the Dalai Lama gave a one-day Buddhist teaching in Oslo. I came into the auditorium ten minutes late and saw a couple storming out and demanding their money back.

But I have also met many who were moved to tears by his sheer presence. A few have felt intense joy after they managed to shake his hand as he walked past. Others were surprised by the little nuggets of insight that hit home with unexpected force.

In 2000, I accompanied the Dalai Lama to Belfast, Northern Ireland, where he first met Richard Moore, the man he called his hero. He gave a speech to a large crowd of Catholics and Protestants, two Christian communities who have been in a state of conflict for many years. He said to them, "When human emotions come out of control, then the best part of the brain where we make judgments cannot function properly. Try to minimize violence, not by force but by awareness and respect. Through dialogue, taking others' interests and then sharing one's own, there's a way to solve the problems."

The Dalai Lama then asked the crowd, "Is this useful? If useful, please remember, and eventually implement. If you feel this too idealistic, not practical, then you forget. No problem."

I thought that was a realistic conclusion to his talk. The Dalai Lama had no illusions that his speech could easily resolve the intractable, generations-old conflict. But he understands that his ability to bring people together, to inspire them to persevere, is a valuable attribute. To bring two communities that have been at war for decades together under one roof, to have a Protestant minister and a Catholic priest standing side by side next to him, was in itself significant.

The wisdom of the Dalai Lama is honed from seven decades of daily spiritual practice and prolonged retreats. He is trained to look at all ideas, including Buddhist teachings, as something offered up for reflection rather than carved in stone. And he is encouraged to retain what is useful and discard what he feels is at odds with reason or experience.

The Dalai Lama's main message is that our goal in life is to be happy. And he says that the path to happiness is through practicing compassion. He says, "All the people, even if they are hostile, are living beings like me who fear suffering and want happiness. They have every right not to suffer, and to achieve happiness. That thought makes us feel deep concern for the well-being of all others. It is the basis of genuine compassion."

But "compassion," like "peace," has become something of a cliché, and many pay lip service to it. Some of its potency and resonance has been lost. This book will focus on the essential nature of compassion, and, at the very least, its power to remind us to do the right thing. The Dalai Lama infuses every moment of his life with compassion, and it is the core message that he wants to convey to the world.

The Dalai Lama's words point the way to living a happier and more meaningful life. Much of what he says is simple, everyday good sense. Adult or child, educated or illiterate, rich or poor— he asks us all to deepen our compassion as a means to genuine well-being. By his example he shows us how to improve our peace of mind, and he hopes that we translate compassion into tangible action.

Part One

OVERCOMING ADVERSITY

External circumstances are not what draw us into suffering. Suffering is caused and permitted by an untamed mind. The appearance of self-defeating emotions in our minds leads us to faulty actions. The naturally pure mind is covered over by these emotions and troubling conceptions. The force of their deceit pushes us into faulty actions, which leads inevitably to suffering. We need, with great awareness and care, to extinguish these problematic attitudes, the way gathering clouds dissolve back into the sphere of the sky. When our self-defeating attitudes, emotions, and conceptions cease, so will the harmful actions arising from them.

—His Holiness the Dalai Lama

THE RED CHAIR

A clay planter sat on an open balcony balustrade a few feet from the Dalai Lama. Within the planter, a bunch of pink and violet plastic flowers, set off by green plastic leaves, were embedded in soil. The flowers looked remarkably real, a bright contrast to the browns and grays of the sheer mountain cliffs that border the Spiti Valley, a place of thin air, muted colors, and isolation. As I watched, the flower petals began to quiver in the wind. Then the green stalks swayed gently. Soon the flowers were buffeted back and forth, bending all the way to one side of the planter before springing back to the other. In a matter of minutes, a gale-force wind had come up, lashing through the constricted corridor formed by the Ki Monastery complex and the eastern ramparts of the valley.

A huge yellow-and-maroon-striped awning had been rigged up over the balcony to protect the Dalai Lama from the bright Spiti sun while he performed the celebrated Kalachakra Empowerment. Suddenly, the sheet of heavy canvas exploded upward with a loud popping sound. The ropes securing two of its corners had torn off cleanly, and the untethered awning flapped ferociously in the wind. The Dalai Lama now stood in sharp relief against the barren, snow-tipped mountains of the Spiti range behind him.

As if punched by a gigantic fist, the awning thudded back down to earth somewhere below the large balcony, narrowly missing the group of Tibetan monks assembled there. Tibetan personnel rushed to the edge of the balcony, leaned far out over the railings, and tried to grab the flailing ropes. An Indian security guard in a bright blue shirt strapped his automatic assault rifle around his torso and reached for a corner of the canvas.

I looked down from the balcony onto the large crowd below. Two thousand Tibetan monks and nuns in maroon robes sat among hundreds of Westerners: tourists, curiosity seekers, students of Tibetan Buddhism. Surrounding them were the pilgrims, mostly ethnic Tibetans from the neighboring regions of Ladakh, Zanskar, and Kinnaur. Everyone watched in fascination as the men wrestled to contain the colorful, gyrating awning. Out of the corner of my eye, I saw something that looked like a white, elongated bird floating through the air above the crowd of monks sitting below. One of them, without moving from his lotus position, had reached inside his satchel and taken out a *khata*—a white ceremonial scarf. He had crumpled it into a ball and thrown it out over the crowd. It sailed through the air gracefully, powered by the wind, in bold contrast to the harshly undulating canvas above. A monk with a long goatee caught the *khata* in midstream, then hurled it farther. In no time, as if by some unseen cue, hundreds of soft silk cloths streaked through the air, forming a shimmering, ever-changing web of white above a sea of red.

But the Dalai Lama's concentration on the text he was reciting was total. He was oblivious to the loud cracking sounds of the awning, the thick ropes lashing madly in front of him, and the *khatas* floating below him.

Ki Monastery sits eleven miles, as the crow flies, from the Tibet border. The Dalai Lama had not been so close to his home country since his exile to India forty years before. The grandeur of the northern Spiti Valley is breathtaking. Spiti is high country, most of its villages located 12,000 feet above sea level. Kibber, a small town to the north, is one of the highest human settlements in the world, at 13,975 feet.

From the spacious balcony of the monastery, I could see a few villages perched far above the Spiti River. They were tiny oases surrounded by fields of barley, peas, and mustard. Their neat, whitewashed houses, grouped in tiers, had thick mud walls and tiny windows—the better to withstand the bitter winters. The flat roofs, used for storage and as work space, were rimmed with stacks of winter firewood and bales of hay. Spiti, closed to foreigners until 1993, is the last of the Shangri-Las, a valley hidden in the high Himalayas at the western tip of the Tibetan plateau.

Rudyard Kipling, more than a century ago, wrote in *Kim*: "At last they came into a world within a world. . . . 'Surely the Gods live here. . . . This is no place for men.'"

The Kalachakra Empowerment in the Spiti Valley, held in August 2000, was the first of the new millennium. At the conclusion of the eleven-day ceremony, serious students of Buddhism would receive permission to begin their study of the Kalachakra Tantra, one of the most elaborate forms of meditation in Tibetan Buddhism. Some practitioners choose this path over others because it promises quick results—the shortest route to enlightenment. For ordinary Tibetans and non-Buddhists, simply attending the Empowerment confers a blessing. And it gives participants the opportunity to offer their own small dose of "positive energy" as a subtle but tangible contribution to world peace. "The previous Dalai Lamas rarely performed the Kalachakra Empowerment," Tsering Dorje, a Tibetan monk in his fifties, told me at the event. "In recent years, the present Dalai Lama has done many in different countries. The ceremony is usually requested during times of uncertainty: declining spirituality, large-scale conflicts. These days, things are getting worse. The world is really in trouble. I wouldn't be surprised if the Dalai Lama has to step up the frequency of these Empowerments."

As the Empowerment ritual began, the Dalai Lama said to the large crowd assembled before him, "I'm very happy, but physically not very fit, because of high altitude I have some headaches. I think you also have similar experience." He shaded his eyes from the sun and peered out at the expectant faces. "I personally put more emphasis and give more importance to the teachings before the actual Empowerment. I always consider them more important, because they are a more or less thorough explanation of Buddhism: how to develop peace of mind and how to have a happy life. After a few days of preliminaries, a lot of complicated rituals follow, and only if you have a good knowledge of Buddhism, you can understand these rituals."

The Dalai Lama went on to reassure the participants that the essentials of the Empowerment are not easy things to grasp, and told them not to worry about it too much. Fundamentally, he said that he believes that the Kalachakra does something good for the world and that the right motivation, genuine spirituality, and positive experience of the Empowerment can make a contribution—at least to the peace of mind of the people who come. And, he added, it may also have a beneficial impact on the local ecology and on the region where the Kalachakra has taken place.

The centerpiece of the Kalachakra Tantra is the magnificent mandala, meticulously created out of colored sand by a team of Tibetan monks working around the clock. It is a pictorial representation of an imaginary castle filled with 722 figures of the Buddha, manifestations of consciousness and reality. The task of these Buddhas is to create a favorable atmosphere that will help reduce tension and violence in the world. During the Empowerment, the Dalai Lama asks participants to visualize themselves as Buddhas and to enter the mandala symbolically with him. He acts as a guide, describing the images and deities that line the convoluted corridors representing the cycles of existence. As they mentally climb up to the high inner center, participants are cleansed like newborn infants and implanted with the seed of a Buddha.

"During the Empowerment, I hope you remember one basic thing," the Dalai Lama told the crowd. "All of us want to be happy. No one wants to suffer. If we act and behave with that in mind, then it will be a good thing that you came."

❧

After the freak wind storm, the Dalai Lama and his retinue of Tibetan monks went into the Mandala Chapel, its back wall dominated by three huge, brightly painted silk scrolls depicting Buddhas. The Dalai Lama moved to one side of a canopied table, the platform on which the colored-sand mandala would be constructed. He was about to perform "Blessing the Ground by Stamping the Feet," an important ceremony in the complicated process of purifying the Kalachakra Empowerment site before the rite could begin.

As the monks chanted in unison, the Dalai Lama did a highly stylized "dance" around the table. With the ritual bell and dagger in his hands, his arms wheeled in opposite directions, drawing large circles in the air. At the same time, he lifted his left foot high before stamping it down with a slight thud in front of his right. He wobbled slightly as he performed the exaggerated cross step. After regaining his balance, he repeated the motions, this time high stepping with his right foot. I knew that each time he lifted one of his feet, the Dalai Lama was visualizing a three-pointed dagger appearing on his sole. And each time he stamped his foot on the ground, he imagined wrathful deities emanating from the dagger to subdue evil influences. Stepping in this way, he slowly completed a ritual circumambulation of the table. The process created an invisible, impregnable circle that purged the space of malignant earth spirits. I sat cross-legged in the small chapel among the fifty monks, listening to their sonorous chanting.

I was mesmerized by this purification ritual, conducted by the Dalai Lama himself—I had heard much about it, but this was the first time I had been able to witness it. And then there was the quality of the light. At 12,600 feet, it had a beautiful clarity not found elsewhere. Filtered by soft yellow curtains, the mountain light entered the spacious Mandala Chapel and bathed the space around the Dalai Lama and those near him in an ethereal gentleness.

Then my agony started. Bodily pain—the nemesis of meditative concentration—broke through to the forefront of my mind. Sitting cross-legged on the floor for more than a short time is an excruciatingly painful undertaking for me. Now my knees were jackknifed, level with my ears, and my hands were clasped so tightly around them that my knuckles had turned white. My back was hunched, and I had strained my neck as far forward as possible to maintain a modicum of balance. The chanting, even the rarely seen ritual dancing, had ceased to soothe. I squirmed and wriggled as I experimented with different postures and my mind desperately cast around for a way to alleviate the pain. My concentration and my equanimity were broken, while the monks next to me sat perfectly immobile, oblivious to my descent into private hell.

The Dalai Lama glanced my way. He spoke briefly to his monk attendant, Paljor-la, who quietly slipped out of the chapel. When he returned, he was carrying a red folding chair. He brought the chair over to me. At first, I was all set to wave the chair away, but then I thought better of it. I knew I could sit cross-legged for only a few more minutes, and then I would have to leave the room. I rose stiffly and sat in the chair. Head and shoulders above the sitting monks, I stuck out like a sore thumb. I was hugely embarrassed, but I also felt humbled. The Dalai Lama had somehow noticed my painful predicament and had taken steps to do something about it. He was acutely attuned to human suffering and exquisitely aware of his surroundings. And his compassion radar is always active, even in the middle of a complicated and demanding days-long ritual.

NOW HERE,
THREE FINGERS

In the center of the small intensive-care ward at the Primary
Children's Hospital in Salt Lake City was a portable unit
crammed with high-tech instruments. Children with a vari-
ety of life-threatening diseases sat on folding chairs around it,
doctors and caregivers squeezed in among them. A few of the
children had shaved heads. Some were connected to IV stands.

In the front row, two preteen girls sat together. They had
dressed up for the occasion. One, a blonde wearing a pink dress,
had fashionable high heels. The other, black-haired, wearing
yellow pants, chewed gum next to her. A stocky boy, perhaps
twelve years old, sat to their right, hooked up to an IV. With both
hands, he held a disposable camera in front of his chest.

The Dalai Lama sat before them and beamed. Clutching the
armrests of his chair for support, he leaned his upper body as far
forward as possible, as if he were about to propel himself from
the chair toward his audience. "Hello, first time," he said to the
thirty-odd children. "You may not have met me before, but,

without introducing one another, we know each other. We're same human being."

He gave his head a little waggle, in the style of the Indians, who shake their heads sideways to indicate agreement. After living in India for more than fifty years, the Dalai Lama has taken on some of the more distinctive mannerisms of the citizens of his adopted country.

"Slight differences: color or size of nose, isn't it?" The Dalai Lama passed his hand along his cheek and then grabbed his nose. He pointed toward one of the girls sitting in the front row. "And hairstyle." She had a full head of frizzy hair. In his eagerness, he half launched himself off the chair.

"When I meet a new person I feel we're old acquaintances, no need for introductions," the Dalai Lama continued. "We're same, same emotional level. I see a smile, teeth. There's no barrier between us. We should therefore approach others openly, recognizing each person just like ourselves. So, on that basis, I want to say hello and then greetings."

It is a hallmark of the Dalai Lama to stress that he treats all people he comes into contact with equally. The reality is a bit more nuanced. I saw him take precious time out of an event in Vancouver to pose for photos with Larry, a homeless man in oversized hand-me-downs, who had waited four hours for a chance to see him. The smiles on both their faces when they held hands were a revelation. On another occasion, outside a hotel in Calgary, he listened to the story of a panhandler. The man was sobbing, overcome with emotion, as they parted. And the Dalai Lama often defies his security guards to dash into a crowd to say a few words of comfort to elderly, disabled, or sick people who have come to see him. I have no doubt that he naturally, instinctively, reaches out to those who need him most.

"Now, you are young people so your life just beginning," the Dalai Lama said to the patients. He was obviously energized by their presence. "Some of you physically a little complicated, but then basically we all have the same brain, same potential, so should not feel some kind of uncomfortable feeling."

Pamela Atkinson, a director of the hospital, sat on the Dalai Lama's right. A patrician-looking woman with gray hair, she wore an eye-catching red blazer over a plaid skirt. She began to tell the Dalai Lama a few things about the ward.

"Some of the children are here for cancer treatment. Some are here for various infections. One boy is here for a heart transplant," Atkinson said. Until this moment, the Dalai Lama had been his usual jovial and perky self, smiling, his face relaxed. But when he heard the words "heart transplant," his body stiffened. As he stared fixedly at the children before him, there was an intensity on his face that had not been there before. Without taking his eyes off them, he leaned his head close to Atkinson's. "Hmmm?"

"One boy is here to have a heart transplant . . . when a heart becomes available," Atkinson repeated.

The short, thick eyebrows of the Dalai Lama inched upward. The horizontal furrows on his brow darkened and deepened— they extended along his entire forehead, wrapped themselves around the sides of his shaved head, ending above his ears. Seemingly, nothing in his face had changed, beyond the slight upward movement of the eyebrows. But it was now a very different Dalai Lama who sat in front of us. In one instant, the smiling face was gone, transformed into one full of latent energy. It was as if everything he had, all his life force, had been summoned and brought to bear on his face. His head began to nod ever so slightly and without a break, like a metronome.

I had never seen the Dalai Lama like this. Not once in all my travels with him. My first thought was: This is what compassion looks like. My second thought: It is amazing how he can project such power and emotion so instantaneously and so effectively through his face. He empathized with the plight of the boy in such a deep, tangible way. Compassion, with a magnitude and ferociousness beyond my comprehension, rose from deep within him and showed clearly on his face. I was mesmerized.

I vaguely heard Atkinson finishing up her description of the ward—". . . different types of diseases and diagnoses," she was saying. "The children come to the hospital from different states—they're not all from Utah." The Dalai Lama's face softened. He started to look around the room and the slight nodding stopped. The spell had been broken.

"Your Holiness, the children would like to ask you some questions. Is this all right?" Atkinson asked.

"Yes, all right," he replied.

A boy of about twelve, standing near the back of the room, said, "My name is Matthew. Some of us have been away from home for quite a while. How do you handle being away from Tibet for so long?"

"There is Tibetan saying," the Dalai Lama answered. "'Wherever you feel at home, is your home.' So if mental atmosphere or surrounding very good, I feel at home. Perhaps this may lead to a deeper philosophical point. I think every day, every morning we take new birth. So therefore, the new birth, where friendly atmosphere exists, then that truly is our home. Now things are relative, there is no absolute, so relative means . . ."

The Dalai Lama raised his left palm level with his face, bent the thumb and index finger down, leaving the other three fingers up.

"Now here, three fingers," he said to the children, with the opening moves of a seasoned magician.

With his right hand he pulled two fingers down, leaving only the ring finger sticking up.

"If you ask, this finger, whether long or short, difficult to say."

He then raised his middle finger alongside the ring finger.

"However, with this, short."

He then compared the ring finger with his pinky.

"With this, long. So long or short is relative. Similarly, when we think about home, it is often in relation to something. You can think about home in relation to your birthplace or home in relation to where you live now. But about the birthplace. If we go more precise, then the very year or month or week, day, and hour and minute where you born that's real home. Otherwise real home always change, isn't it?"

The Dalai Lama looked at Matthew, not really expecting an answer.

"Yeah," Matthew mumbled uncertainly.

"So it is by thinking various viewpoints, their relative nature, that you can develop some kind of feeling of home wherever there is some positive facility there. Of course, if home or if things are something absolute, then it won't change even if we look at it from different angle. But things are relative. Therefore looking from different angles we get different picture.

"Some sense?" the Dalai Lama asked Matthew and then, without waiting for an answer, burst into laughter.

The Dalai Lama was speaking about his own notion of home. He has a different attitude about it than most people I know. He has said that he is at home wherever he is, as long as the conditions are favorable, as long as he is not in a hostile environment. Because of his years of scholarly studies, his mind is of a very rigorous, analytic bent. He examined the question of what exactly constitutes "home." The home or hospital where we were born? This could be different from the place where we grew up. Which place is the real "home"?

The idea that there are no absolutes, that things do not exist absolutely, independently, is fundamental to the Dalai Lama's worldview. He once explained this idea using a black mug as an example. "What exactly is this mug? We're seeing color, shape. But if we take away shape, color, material, what is mug? Where is mug? This mug is a combination of particles, atoms, quarks. But each particle not 'mug.' The same can be said of everything. Including yourself. The mug, 'me,' are merely labels, something we use to describe everyday reality. The mug, 'me,' came into existence because of a complex web of causes and conditions. They do not exist independently."

But what has this got to do with real life? For the Dalai Lama, perspective is everything. Much of our unhappiness, our suffering, is caused by discrepancies between our perceptions and what is real. Because of lifelong conditioning, the idea that there is a sharp distinction between ourselves and others is ingrained in us. Self-interest makes sense from this self-centered perspective.

As a result of decades of spiritual practice, the Dalai Lama has come to realize, through direct experience rather than intellectual abstraction, that his existence, like that of the mug, is dependent on an infinite, intricately linked series of events, people, causes, and conditions. He believes that there is a fundamental interconnectedness between people and people, and between people and things. He has no doubt that "his" interest and "your" interest are inextricably connected.

The Dalai Lama's beliefs have an influence on his attitude and, by extension, on his behavior. As a Buddhist, he has dedicated his life to the alleviation of suffering. And he knows that major causes of suffering are our inflated egos, a heightened sense of our own importance, our selfish needs. This sense of me, me, and me. Our overattachment to our wants, our needs. Therefore, any change of perception that leads to a more balanced view of our ego and the world around us is helpful to our mental well-being.

One of the girls in the front row said to the Dalai Lama, "My name is Natalie Burdick. I'm just wondering if you believe that spirit helps people get healed."

A nurse sitting next to me whispered, "Natalie is thirteen. She has leukemia."

"I believe we can benefit through prayers," the Dalai Lama

replied. "But as far as some people having healing powers, I'm skeptical."

He placed his palm just above Atkinson's hand and moved it around in circles.

"Hand go like that and then cured, that I think very difficult," he said. "Unless . . . you know . . . itching." The Dalai Lama scratched his right forearm, then the inside elbow. "Here also, always itching." He bent his head to show his audience the bare skin on the back of his neck.

"Eczema," he explained. "So if someone comes and heals this itching within minutes, so complete cure. Then I believe. Till that happens, I'm skeptical." His booming laugh resounded in the ward.

After he caught his breath, he smiled at Natalie and continued. "I think the main thing is human compassion. It gives us freshness and more positive feelings. That very important, very helpful. Compassion causes positive transformation within our bodies. Through that way, healing takes place."

This physical transformation has been demonstrated in the laboratory by two prominent scientists, Richard Davidson and Jon Kabat-Zinn. As part of an experiment, they trained a group of stressed-out biotech workers in compassion meditation. Subsequent brain scans showed that the meditators' anxiety had decreased. The participants were also injected with a flu vaccine as part of the study. Their blood was then tested to measure the level of antibodies they had produced. The results? After eight weeks of meditation, their immune systems were noticeably enhanced.

For the Dalai Lama, cultivating compassion is a key to spiritual development. He believes that by enhancing compassion, not only do we show kindness toward others, but we ourselves actually feel happier. One prayer that he has recited on a daily basis for the last seven decades of his life goes like this: "For as long as space exists and sentient beings endure, may I, too, remain to dispel the misery of the world." I have seen him break into tears as he recited this in front of large crowds. The sense of promise and commitment implied in the verse is firmly embedded in every fiber of his being. And it is remarkable that, after all those years, the prayer still holds the power to move and inspire him in such a profound manner.

The Dalai Lama said to me on another occasion, "It is important to consider others at least as important as ourselves. This is essence of spirituality. Extending compassion to others does not mean self-sacrifice, something that benefits only others. It is not like tax, or burden loaded onto our shoulders. This is mistake! Think about it, from your own experience. If you feel compassion, you also feel stronger determination. Whether this attitude brings benefit to others, not sure, but you can for sure feel better."

Another girl in the front row asked the Dalai Lama, "I'm just wondering, we all have trials and stuff, but how do you get through things like that and stay so happy?"

"Yes, there are some difficulties. The other day I mentioned more than seven billion people on this planet. I think no single person who has no problems. But then the important thing is one's own attitude toward these problems. I think with my own close friends, some people, with same circumstances, always complain, complain. Others obviously have a lot of problems, too. But for them, very, very little complaint. So that shows one's own attitude."

He thought for a moment, then added, "When dealing with problems, it is useful to look at various angles, then very often the problems become more manageable."

Atkinson had been looking at her watch with increasing frequency. She was obviously worried that the Dalai Lama's reluctance to leave would cause him to be late for his next appointment. He was fully engaged with this room full of young people. Although I have traveled extensively with the Dalai Lama, this was the first time I had seen him interact with a group of very sick children. The exchanges were animated and the chemistry was palpable. His answers to their questions were rather surprising, though. He didn't shy away from explaining some of the deeper philosophical concepts to these young people. His rational, logic-driven character was clearly on display and he was not talking down to them in any way.

"Now we must go into the other room, with younger children," Atkinson finally told the Dalai Lama.

Natalie Burdick raised her hand again and in a small voice said to Atkinson, "I just wonder if I would be able to shake his hand."

"I'll come," the Dalai Lama said without any hesitation. He stood up and walked over. "I come here and we take some pictures."

One of the girls in the front row stood up and gave him her chair. He sat down and said, "Now come here." He patted his knee and pulled her down so that she was sitting on his lap. The room was now in an uproar; many of the kids were yelling with delight. The Dalai Lama put his left arm around Natalie and pulled her down on his lap as well. Both girls were grinning widely. A dozen photographers rushed to the front to capture the moment.

The Dalai Lama turned around in his chair and pointed to a young boy of about ten, farther back. "The small one. The small one," he said.

The boy approached hesitantly. His right eye was closed, and part of his head was shaved. An angry scar traced a large arc from the top of his skull to the bottom of his right ear. He had obviously had serious surgery not too long ago.

"Come here, come here," the Dalai Lama said to the boy. His voice was suddenly a high-pitched coo, strikingly different from his usual baritone. This is what he calls his "goat" voice, and he seldom uses it.

The Dalai Lama sat the small boy on his lap and put both arms around him. There were more bursts of flashes. He peered closely at the boy and gently touched the scar. "You have some operation here, isn't it?" The boy didn't reply. He was embarrassed by all this attention.

"Ha, ha, ha. Beautiful, beautiful," the Dalai Lama said as the boy got up from his lap. He peered at him closely, with unmistakable concern, grabbed his hand and shook it gently. Then he got up from his chair, put his face next to the boy's, wrapped his arm around the boy's skinny chest, and hugged him with intensity.

Then it was time to go to the next ward.

A MATTER OF KARMA

The Dalai Lama slowly made his way into another ward of Salt Lake City's Primary Children's Hospital. This one was reserved for younger children, most of them under the age of twelve. There were about twenty of them, many either in wheelchairs or hooked up to a bewildering array of electronic devices. Three or four lay on gurneys that had been wheeled into the room, and most had family members or medical workers by their side.

It was standing room only. I was jostled this way and that as I tried to follow the Dalai Lama. Many doctors and caregivers from other parts of the hospital had stationed themselves in the ward very early on, intent on not missing the chance to catch a glimpse of the world-famous monk. A large contingent of photographers, videographers, and reporters jockeyed for the best positions. Half a dozen State Department security agents in suits and with earpieces followed the Dalai Lama closely. A couple of maroon-robed monks, his personal attendants, hovered nearby.

The Dalai Lama went up to a small African-American boy sitting on his mother's lap. She looked up and said, "He is twelve and he has sickle-cell anemia."

The Dalai Lama had trouble understanding and turned to his private secretary, Tenzin Geyche Tethong. He didn't understand either; he approached the woman and leaned close to her.

"Sickle-cell anemia," she repeated.

"What's that?" asked Tethong.

"It's a blood disorder," she said. Her face was contorted; she was holding back tears.

The Dalai Lama turned and peered at the boy again, the expression on his face one of grave concern.

Next to them was a frail boy sitting in a wheelchair, his lap covered by a red blanket. His fair skin was blotched by dark lesions. Large, angry patches disfigured one side of his face and an entire ear; his lips were completely black. Hooked up to a complex of monitors and instruments, the boy waved tentatively at the Dalai Lama, who bent down close and put his hands on the boy's arms. He murmured some indistinct words of comfort and the boy sat up a bit straighter.

The Dalai Lama walked to the other end of the ward. A couple of small children, unable to sit up, lay prone on portable beds. He went to one child and stared down at the tubes protruding from his chest. A nurse introduced the boy: "This is Justin." The Dalai Lama then put his hand on the crown of the boy's head, leaned down, and held his forehead against the child's forehead for a brief moment.

After making his rounds, the Dalai Lama went to the front of the room and sat down next to Pamela Atkinson. It was time for questions.

From the back of the room, a slight man of about thirty, prematurely bald, asked the Dalai Lama in a quavering voice, "What does Buddhism believe about children with disabilities?" His son, swaddled in a green quilt, lay motionless on his lap.

As he asked the question, he thumped the chest of his child several times with unintended force. His eyes never left the Tibetan's face. The child, perhaps five or six years old, seemed unresponsive, his head lolling listlessly to one side.

The Dalai Lama replied through Thupten Jinpa, his longtime Tibetan translator.

"Buddhism . . . in Tibetan society, people with disabilities, particularly children, are considered to be special objects of care and concern. However, from the point of view of the individual . . ." Jinpa translated.

The Dalai Lama decided to speak to the father directly, in English, "In Buddhism, we believe in rebirth, life after life. There is the strong belief that today's unfortunate things happen because of one's own previous karmic . . . uh, wrongdoing."

The father thumped his son a few more times. Then he swallowed and, with a conscious effort, looked away from the Dalai Lama. These clearly weren't the words of comfort he had hoped for. I was also taken aback by the Dalai Lama's response. He is usually very circumspect when he explains quintessentially Buddhist concepts like karma to Westerners, as they can easily be misinterpreted.

The Dalai Lama knew that his response was no consolation

to the father. He knew that it must be difficult for the father to hear that, according to Buddhist teachings, his child's disability was the result of bad deeds committed in a previous life.

The last thing the Dalai Lama wanted was to cause additional pain. But he also did not want to say something trite, something he would consider a meaningless pleasantry. He is always honest, sometimes to the point of being blunt. He is also courageous, ready to dispense tough love if the situation demands it. No dissembling. No short-term avoidance of pain. Facing suffering unflinchingly in the here and now provides a window of opportunity for meaningful transformation. In this case, he simply answered the question as well as he could, given the pressure of time. But I have no doubt he was keenly aware of the distress it caused.

Buddhist philosophy is thoroughly fused with the person of the Dalai Lama. It informs his worldview, his moral universe. His understanding of karma is not the simplistic view of cause and effect that we usually associate with the word. Karma, for him, is weighted with subtle layers of doctrinal implication. But he finds it awkward to explain this to laypeople, who tend to expect short, easy answers.

✧

In a previous talk, given to Tibetan Buddhists, the Dalai Lama stated that what makes karma unique is that it involves intentional action—a desire to do good or cause harm.

There are three different types of action that produce three different types of effects, he told them. Actions that produce suffering and pain are generally considered negative actions. Actions that lead to desirable consequences, such as experiences of joy and happiness, are considered positive actions. The third category includes actions that lead to experiences of neutral feelings. These are neither virtuous nor non-virtuous. Leading a disciplined life and avoiding harmful action is what Buddhists understand as an ethical way of life.

The Dalai Lama also knows that the karmic results of our actions are not immediately obvious. They often show up after a long gestation period. And it becomes very difficult, even impossible, to tell which action caused which result. Action from a previous life could create havoc in this life, for example. But who can remember his or her past life? Who can pin a specific action on a particular result? We can have an intellectual understanding of karma, but we don't have any reliable direct experience of it.

In an earlier interview, the Dalai Lama said something to me that took me by surprise. He said that the suffering experienced by Tibetan people at the hands of the Chinese was, and is, a consequence of past negative actions. A kind of collective cultural karma.

He told me that I should not think of suffering as punishment. There is no deity, no God in Buddhism to mete out punishment. Karma is simply a matter of negative actions that inevitably result in future suffering. For Buddhists, the "law" of karma, like that of gravity, is a natural law. If you put your hand in a flame, no one would suggest that the flame is punishing you when you get burned. The Dalai Lama does not believe that dis-

abled or disadvantaged people "deserve" to be in the unfortunate position they are in or that they are being divinely punished.
There is no doubt that he has profound compassion for all who
suffer, no matter what past negative deeds might have caused
their present suffering.

The Dalai Lama knew that the situation of the father and his
son in this hospital ward was extremely difficult. But he also understood that if the father could somehow look at the circumstances from a Buddhist point of view, from a very different
perspective, he could potentially derive some relief from his
mental anguish. It could even give both father and son an opportunity to achieve a state of grace.

For the father, the sick child provided a chance to reach deep
inside to access a previously unknown reservoir of compassion
and patience. He would need this to nurture his son with loving
care. It would allow him to place the welfare of another person
entirely before his own. And for the Dalai Lama, this opportunity is precious. He believes that it is the path to a deep sense of
joy and satisfaction.

For the son, it was a blessing to have a father who was so caring, so devoted. The father had most certainly been trauma-
tized when he was first confronted with his child's illness and
disability. But after emerging from this dark place, his relationship with his son could grow deeper. He had a chance to learn to
love unconditionally. For the son to experience this love, this
profound sense of affection, was a gift of immense proportions.

The Dalai Lama was deep in thought as he sat at the front of
the ward with the director of the hospital. I believe that he was

troubled by the brief interchange with the father. He swiveled in his chair, trying to get a good view of the son.

"Belief in the karmic theory helps provide some sense of acceptance," he said finally. "In Buddhism, karma means cause and effect. Suffering unavoidable. It is something we have to deal with. Accepting the situation decreases anxiety. Acceptance gives peace of mind. Also, there are different disabilities. If disabilities purely physical, then maybe no major difficulties. Because thinking capabilities still there."

Suddenly the Dalai Lama got up and started to weave his way to the back of the ward, toward the father and son. The father saw him approaching and smiled tentatively—there was anticipation in his eyes.

The Dalai Lama, however, had something else in mind. Maybe he meant to get a closer look at the boy but sensed that he couldn't give any meaningful comfort. Whatever the reason, he went to another boy sitting in a wheelchair next to them. His mother was behind him, one arm wrapped around his chest. The Dalai Lama touched him carefully on the shoulder. The child looked down at the floor; he did not respond. The Dalai Lama gently smoothed his tuft of unruly hair back in place. He then walked back to his chair. He did not look at the father and his disabled son.

The Dalai Lama decided to address the entire group. "What is important is that you are receiving treatment, and in an environment where there is tremendous affection. This provides a wonderful basis for healing to take place. I'm so happy to learn that here parents have the opportunity to be with their children. Children can therefore feel at home, feel secure. This will definitely contribute toward the healing process. Of course the parents certainly have very painful feelings, they sharing in the suffering."

He took in the crowded room, jam-packed with high-tech medical equipment, and the sick children and the horde of curious, protective adults. His eyes registered unmistakable concern as they lingered on the boy with skin lesions.

"Buddhists, as I mentioned earlier, they believe in the concept of karma," he continued after a long pause. "Every event, every experience, happens due to our own previous action. So for them, thinking along this line, then sometimes they have less worry, less pain. For those who have no particular faith, then perhaps they can think another way: Out of six billion human beings, many have similar kinds of problems, but in many cases, they have no one to take care. No medical facilities. So if they think this way, they may feel less lonely. They may think that they are fortunate to have this level of support."

A small boy of about eight sat in a red toy car near the front. His mother whispered something in his ear. He put a finger on his lips, shushing her.

"What is your favorite food?" a girl sitting in a wheelchair asked the Dalai Lama hesitantly. She had one tube in her nose and another coming out of one wrist. Her doctor, a young woman sitting close behind her, beamed with pleasure at her question.

"If I'm hungry, then all food very good."

Everyone in the room laughed, grateful for the diversion.

"Yesterday and also day before yesterday, very hectic programs," the Dalai Lama continued. "My breakfast very early, usually five-thirty. I get up three-thirty these days. My breakfast five-thirty, so then around twelve, my stomach empty." He patted his stomach a few times.

The girl was delighted by his answer.

"But then more precise, I think usually I prefer flour than rice," the Dalai Lama said. "I think this maybe my birth area. Right from the beginning, breakfast we always consume bread. Varieties of bread. Especially my mother. My mother, expert. She made different breads. So I think her children spoiled by her expertise."

Atkinson said, "Thank you, great question. Anybody else?"

But the Dalai Lama was not finished.

"One time . . ." he began in English, and then decided to switch to Tibetan, relating an anecdote directly to the Tibetans in his entourage. He was enjoying himself, interrupting his story with peals of giggles from time to time.

Thupten Jinpa translated for the group: "This reminds His Holiness of the story of when he was once traveling in Ladakh— a very high plateau in the Himalayas, very dry and dusty. They had been driving for hours and finally they had to stop to take a rest. Accompanying His Holiness was an Indian doctor who was sent by the government of India. The doctor was so hungry that as they stopped he took out a Tibetan cookie and devoured it. His Holiness asked him if it was good, and the doctor said without any hesitation that when you are hungry even a piece of stone would taste good."

A woman, in a voice laden with grief, asked, "Your Holiness, thank you for being here. My son lost his leg six days ago." She had dark brown hair and was sitting directly behind her pale son. She had a hard time suppressing her tears. "It is so wonderful you came here. My son wants to ask you, he is too shy to ask himself, if at some point in your life you'd be able to return to your homeland?"

The Dalai Lama looked over to her and her son, his face suffused with sympathy.

"I'm quite sure, quite sure," he replied with unshakable conviction. "Although at present, things are almost hopeless, but things are changing. I think global level, also in PRC [People's Republic of China] itself, things are moving, changing." The Dalai Lama's forefinger described circles in the air. "In any case, in modern times, especially now twenty-first century, the totalitarian regimes no future. That's certain. People of PRC itself, I think, now lost faith toward Communist ideology. Now today, all these Communists without faith of Communism."

He started to laugh at the idea of this incongruity.

"Actually any political party with their own ideology, the party members must have firm faith towards that ideology." He had a tough time controlling his laughter and had difficulty finishing the sentence. "But in China's case I think . . . ha ha ha . . . big contradiction. So therefore things are changing. Things are changing."

Atkinson said to the room, "We have one final question."

The boy with the lesions on his skin raised his hand. A tube had been inserted into a nostril; his face was a kaleidoscope of black and red blotches.

"What is your favorite memory of your family?" he said.

"Of course, no doubt with my mother," the Dalai Lama replied. "Very gentle, very kind. And as I mentioned earlier always prepare good food for her children. Then perhaps I think my immediate elder brother, now no longer with us, he already passed away. We spent years together; we grew up together. I have much affection and love for him and he in turn had much affection for me."

A hint of sadness flitted across the Dalai Lama's face as he talked about his deceased brother, Samten Taklha, who died young and unexpectedly.

"But then my father, very short-tempered," he said, and burst into laughter. It was fascinating to see his mood change in a heartbeat, from a palpable sense of loss to uninhibited mirth.

"My father has good mustache," he said, running his finger along his upper lip. "So one day I tried to pull . . . and my father immediately lost temper and hit."

To everyone's surprise, he proceeded to illustrate this by hitting his cheek resoundingly with his hand and then clapping a startled Atkinson on the knee.

The Dalai Lama had been closer to his mother than his father. But while he lived as a young monk in Lhasa, he saw his father quite often; they both made it a point to attend the daily tea ceremony with other monk officials. His father loved his horses and fed them eggs and tea before he himself had breakfast, and before he called on his son.

"Another occasion . . . my father very fond of pork." The

Dalai Lama had some difficulty with pronouncing the word. It came out sounding like "bork." Atkinson was confused.

"Pork, pork," the Dalai Lama repeated for her benefit.

"I already became Dalai Lama," he continued. "So, according to tradition, young lama should not eat pork, egg, or fish. Should avoid. So Dalai Lama's kitchen, from my own kitchen, no serving pork. Occasionally, when my father enjoy pork, I sit just behind him, like dog." To demonstrate, he lifted his shoulders and raised both his drooping hands to his chest, mimicking a begging puppy.

"Then occasionally he don't care about tradition, my father gives me little pieces of pork," he concluded.

Atkinson thanked the Dalai Lama and told the gathering that he had to leave to go to another engagement.

As he stood up, a small boy asked him, "Do you wear the same clothes every day?"

"Yes, this is monk's robe, it is comfortable," he answered.

"When feel heat, warm, like this," he said, and began to unwrap his maroon outer shawl.

"Cold, like this," he said, pulling the shawl over his shoulders.

"And further cold—" He hunched his shoulders and hitched the wool cloth up over his head for a moment so that it completely covered his head and face.

The crowd laughed together as the Dalai Lama made his way out of the ward.

THE WRONG END
OF THE BINOCULARS

I first met Paul Ekman over a decade ago. I found him to be empathic, a polymath, and all-around good company. He drove a fancy two-seater convertible and wore colorful shoelaces. He was sixty-seven at the time and was considered the world's preeminent scientist in the study of facial expressions.

But I had also heard that if I had met him even a few months earlier, before he went to the Himalayas, I would have found him an absolute boor. Ekman had been loud, aggressive, and bad-tempered, and his reputation had preceded him wherever he went. His colleagues, his students, and his family were all used to treating him warily. They never knew when he would fly off into one of his legendary, explosive fits of anger.

All that changed when he had a pivotal meeting with the Dalai Lama in Dharamsala, India, one spring day in 2000.

Ekman had never met the Dalai Lama before. He came reluctantly and with a great deal of cynicism to the Mind & Life Institute's conference, held inside the residence of the Dalai Lama, for a three-day dialogue on destructive emotions.

Ekman was the odd man out. Unlike his six colleagues, he was less than enthusiastic about spending time with the Dalai Lama. Ekman knew very little about him and felt he had nothing to learn from Eastern wisdom traditions like Buddhism. He had little use for religion, as he had dedicated his life to scientific inquiry.

B. Alan Wallace, a close friend of the Dalai Lama's and one of the participants in the conference, had serious misgivings about including Ekman. He didn't doubt his brilliance, but Wallace was convinced that the organizers had made a terrible mistake in inviting Ekman; he was so closed-minded about Buddhism that it was inconceivable that he would be able to contribute constructively to the discussions.

Paul Ekman is a psychologist whose groundbreaking work has helped define the science of emotions. Over the years, he has become the world's most famous face reader, an expert in the detection of lies. He is much in demand by the FBI, the CIA, and the U.S. Transportation Security Administration. Antiterrorist investigators and police forces call on him regularly. They want him not only to help solve critical cases, but also to teach them how to tell accurately when someone is lying.

Ekman has held lie-detecting workshops for lawyers, poker players, and even paranoid spouses. More than five hundred people worldwide have gone through the rigorous process of learning to use his detailed research protocol, the Facial Action Coding

System, or FACS. Using FACS, an investigator is able to pinpoint exactly which of the forty-three facial muscles are deployed at any given moment, even micro-expressions or transient emotional cues that last only fractions of a second. It is an effective and proven method of identifying people who are under stress or trying to deceive.

Dr. Cal Lightman, the central character in the TV series *Lie to Me*, was based on Ekman. In the series, Lightman, played by the actor Tim Roth, is a brilliant human polygraph with expertise in micro-expressions and body language. Having spent decades reading faces, he assists law enforcement agencies in their criminal investigations, using applied psychology.

Ekman had come to the Dharamsala conference because of his daughter, with whom he shares a very strong bond. Eve is his only daughter, born when he was nearly fifty years old. The young woman, twenty years old at the time of the conference, was fascinated by the Tibetans she had met while living in Nepal as a student, and was eager to visit the home of the Dalai Lama.

On the third day of the conference, as the scientists and observers left the cramped conference hall for a tea break, Ekman saw his chance to introduce Eve to the Dalai Lama. After an hour and a half of focused dialogue, most participants went straight out to the enclosed balcony to relax and enjoy tea and biscuits and the great views of the wooded grounds outside the Dalai Lama's residence.

Instead of joining his colleagues, Ekman steered his nervous daughter forward to the Dalai Lama, who, alone among the eighty-some people in the conference, seemed not to need any breaks. He continued to sit cross-legged in his armchair. His long-time translator, Thupten Jinpa, hovered nearby, making sure the Dalai Lama had a full mug of hot water and some cookies.

Eve, like her father, is usually anything but shy. She is outgoing and vivacious, and embraces life full-on. But on this day in Dharamsala she was strangely unsure of herself. She found herself out of her depth in this exclusive gathering of leading scientists and spiritually accomplished people. And she was mortified by the prospect of actually meeting and speaking to the Dalai Lama.

Father and daughter sat down in the armchairs on either side of the Tibetan.

"This is my daughter," Ekman said to the Dalai Lama. "And she is my spiritual leader. She is the reason I came to this meeting and I'm very grateful for that. It was her interest in Tibet that led me to say to the Mind & Life Institute, 'If you have a meeting, I want you to invite me, because I want to be able to bring my daughter and have her in the Dalai Lama's presence.' I thought there is no better gift I can give to her."

Ekman explained that Eve had spent some time living in a Tibetan refugee camp in Nepal when she was fifteen years old, and that because of that experience she was very concerned about the welfare of exiled Tibetans. He said she wanted to ask him a personal question. The Dalai Lama beamed at Eve. He reached over and held Ekman's hand while he waited.

"I wanted to know why we get the angriest at those we are in love with," Eve said.

The Dalai Lama pondered the question for a moment and

then told her that we tend to expect too much from the people who are close to us. We develop unrealistic expectations and project nonexistent qualities onto them. He told her that a more pragmatic approach is simply to accept their flaws. This would lessen potential disappointment and reduce anger.

For the duration of this short exchange, the Dalai Lama inexplicably held on to Ekman's hand.

"I never said another word after introducing Eve, but I had two unusual experiences," Ekman shared with the Dalai Lama some years later. "One was that during the entire ten minutes I was filled with a feeling of physical warmth. It was not a metaphor; it was real warmth. I had a very strong physical sensation for which I do not have an English word—it comes closest to 'warmth,' but there was no heat. It felt very, very good, very embracing. You were only holding my hand. It was like nothing I had felt before or after."

"The other unusual experience I had was almost a hallucination," Ekman continued. "We were in the conference room and there were other people waiting for a chance to talk to you. I had this visual impression that Eve and I and you were encapsulated. Looking out into the room was like looking at the world through the wrong end of the binoculars. Although people were quite close, maybe four feet away, it appeared to me as if they were hundreds of feet away."

"Sometimes you actually experience that kind of vision— distant vision," the Dalai Lama replied.

"It was as if the three of us were tightly bound together, and everyone else was off in the distance," Ekman said. "As a scientist, I do not know how to explain it. But that does not mean it is not susceptible to scientific explanation. I just do not know where to start."

Intense bouts of anger had been a regular characteristic in Ekman's life. He had been beaten regularly by his father when he was growing up. The debilitating cycles of out-of-control anger began shortly after the last time his father hit him. He had been eighteen years old. And he warned his father that if he ever hit him again, he would hit back. His father was so unnerved by the menace in his voice that he called the police. Ekman left home forever, his anger clinging to him tightly.

But after that episode with the Dalai Lama, something in Ekman changed.

He began to notice things. For the first couple of days of the conference, he had found many of the discussions irritating. Some were so academic that he felt them to be a waste of his and the Dalai Lama's time. Now he no longer felt impatient about the way the meeting was going.

On the last day of the conference, the Dalai Lama said to the group, "Is this just going to be for good karma, nice conversation, or is anything going to happen?" The Dalai Lama had wanted to know if secularized Buddhist practices would be helpful to Westerners, especially those who have significant issues with "destructive" emotions such as anger, hatred, and depression.

Ekman told me afterward, "He was looking straight at me. I was looking at him. And as he was talking, I was thinking of an appropriate response. It occurred to me to take this on. I felt he was asking me to do this, to make sure it wasn't just talk."

To many participants' surprise, Ekman and Wallace, despite their initial antipathy, decided to take up the Dalai Lama's challenge and collaborate in a pilot study. For more than 2,500 years, Buddhism has refined meditation techniques that have proven to be effective in promoting compassion, kindness, and other positive states of mind. In the West, many scientific studies have focused on altruism, empathy, and other pro-social behaviors that are related to compassion. But amazingly, there have been almost no studies on mental training that could demonstrably increase compassion.

Ekman and Wallace got together and developed a training program that integrated Buddhist contemplative practices with Western techniques for dealing with negative emotional experiences. Their hope was that those enrolled in the training would see their harmful emotional responses diminish and find their compassion and empathy enhanced. They called their research project "Cultivating Emotional Balance in Challenging Times."

After Dharamsala, Ekman traveled to Delhi and met up with his wife, Mary Ann. They had planned a two-week vacation to see parts of India. She noticed the change in him right away. He was much less confrontational. He was downright mellow.

She said to him, "You are acting like a man in love. You are acting so differently. I don't know whether I want you to be changed. You are not the man I married."

It took Mary Ann some time to digest this transformation. Two days later, she said to Ekman, "I'm so grateful. In the last two days you have not had one moment, one incident, of impatience or anger. You are so much easier to be with."

Recently, Ekman said to me, "I do get angry still. But not very often. Much less often than in the previous seven decades. I still have to work on it a little bit. But before Dharamsala, in a typical year, I'd had a hundred angry episodes that I regretted. Now, I may have five or six."

After his first meeting with the Dalai Lama, Ekman, like me, sought out the Tibetan leader at every chance. His continuing research on emotions began to be heavily influenced by what the Dalai Lama calls "science of mind."

Ekman has puzzled over his strange transformation in Dharamsala and has tried to make sense of what happened. He told the Dalai Lama about his lifelong struggle with anger, that he sought the help of psychiatrists from time to time, and that nothing had helped. The encounter in Dharamsala was a turning point. As a scientist, Ekman could not ignore what he had experienced.

Ekman told me that it was frustrating to try to get the Dalai Lama to talk about this experience. As usual, the Tibetan leader refused to admit that he has any kind of magical healing power. Eventually, Ekman offered his own interpretation. He said to the Dalai Lama, "I believe that when people suffer from emotional wounds that they are struggling to deal with, you can somehow direct, radiate, a 'goodness' to the person. It starts with a physical sensation, a warmth that is palpable. It is transformative, at least for some time. Science has no explanation for this. But just because I can't explain it doesn't mean it is not real."

Ekman said that when he first received his Ph.D. some five decades ago, there were a lot of things that scientists could not explain. Now they can. But although much progress has been made, there are still important issues that are not understood. Ekman believes that we are nearing a threshold, and that in the not-too-distant future, scientists will be able to solve some of these enduring mysteries.

Ekman had the feeling that he had known the Dalai Lama all his life. "I believe we were brothers in a previous life," he told me. "I feel that he is the younger brother I never had. I know he isn't, but it feels that way. I worry about him. If he and I are alive fifty years from now, I'm sure scientists will have an explanation about all this. But for now the Dalai Lama is not willing to talk about it."

However, the Dalai Lama did tell Ekman that, although what happened was mysterious, one of the characteristics of mysteries is that they are not untrue. The Dalai Lama said it seems that there was a karmic link between them in the past, from some previous life. "But I'm not a Buddhist," Ekman told me. "The Dalai Lama doesn't want me to be a Buddhist; he does not proselytize. So I listen, and I respect what he says. But I don't necessarily believe it."

In his home, Ekman has half a dozen photos of the Dalai Lama and him together, holding hands and laughing. "When I walk by," he told me, "I look at them, pause for a moment, and re-experience the feeling I had in Dharamsala. Every time. I can't explain it. People simply like to be in his presence. And it is not because his words are wonderful. When he is teaching, he often does so from a Buddhist text and it is difficult to understand. He emanates goodness. Of course, not everyone has the same intense experience as I had. But most people who are within ten or twenty feet of him feel good. Can't explain it scientifically. He can affect people without saying a single word. When you eat a piece of chocolate, it tastes good, but can you explain why it tastes good?"

Ekman also told the Dalai Lama that he believes that there is something about contemplative practices that generates a "goodness" in some people. He could not think of another word to describe it. He says it is a goodness that benefits others. He told me that the Dalai Lama had said to him, "Something mysterious happened. Okay. It is positive. It is good. But these things are not connected to science. Scientists would not have much to say about these strange things. They are my business. They are not for you scientists."

EX-PRISONERS,
TERRORISTS, AND
A MURDERER

I t was a lovely fall day, in September 2003, with temperatures in the mid-eighties. I left my backpacker hotel on Forty-third Street in Manhattan and managed to flag down a cab near Times Square. I had been invited to attend an unusual event with the Dalai Lama, and I wanted to be there with plenty of time to spare. As the cab crawled along Forty-second Street, I was startled to see a giant Dalai Lama smiling benignly down at me from a huge photo that took up the entire front of a four-story building. It was a striking image. He looked straight into the camera with his hands clasped loosely in front of his stomach, his splayed feet in simple plastic flip-flops. It was an advertisement for his public talk, scheduled for the following Sunday in Central Park.

The cab dropped me off at The Mark, a boutique hotel tucked away on Seventy-seventh Street, not far from the park and the Metropolitan Museum of Art. The Dalai Lama had finished an earlier engagement in the city and had rushed back to the hotel to meet with eighteen ex-prisoners.

Jack Kornfield, a former Buddhist monk who holds a Ph.D. in clinical psychology, was waiting in one of the function rooms of the hotel. He would facilitate the one-of-a-kind conversation. The Dalai Lama entered the room and walked up to Kornfield. The two bowed deeply to each other and held hands. The former prisoners and the organizers of the meeting sat in rows facing them.

Kornfield, dressed in his trademark brown vest and open-necked white shirt, said to the Dalai Lama, "There are six million people who are in the American prison system, about as many as there are people in Tibet. Over two million are actually in prisons at any one time. The rest are out on parole. If you are born in the wrong race or the wrong color, if you are a black American, you are five times more likely to end up in prison than in college."

The Dalai Lama listened raptly, fascinated by this aspect of American society about which he knew little. He unwrapped his maroon outer shawl and bundled it around his waist, creating an impression of someone with an outsized potbelly.

Kornfield consulted a clipboard on his lap and continued, "We are meeting today with a group of people who have spent years in prison and have found that they were able to transform themselves, change their hearts. Some are actually involved in projects to help other prisoners."

"Very good, very good." The Dalai Lama nodded.

"My name is Luz Santana. I am an ex-prisoner," a woman sitting in the front row said. "I spent eleven years in a New York State maximum-security prison and I went through all kinds of deprivation and pain. It made me angry. And when I was angry I fought against the system. It started out violent but then it turned calmer. Eventually, the governor granted me clemency, cut my time, and let me go. I was involved in a lot of reform in the prison, a lot of changes in the system—"

"What was the original sentence?" the Dalai Lama interrupted.

"Twenty years. When I finally got out of prison, I worked in the community. Then they wanted me to go back to work inside. And I've been working in the prison for the last eleven years, as a counselor."

The Dalai Lama was not quite sure what the word "counselor" meant and had a brief exchange with his translator, Thupten Jinpa.

"I try to teach women prisoners the things that I learned to keep myself sane and healthy," Santana continued. "Things that made me more caring, more loving. That's what I do for a living."

"Very good, good story," the Dalai Lama said. "I think this is clear indication that everyone has potential to do good. I think much depends on one's own awareness, one's inner quality. And also I think it's important to know the very nature of human mind, which is always changing, moment by moment. Depending on the situation, it is possible for a complete change of direction."

"I believe everyone is good," Santana said.

"True," the Dalai Lama agreed.

"But that circumstances make them act out badly."

"I think true," the Dalai Lama said. "When we born, everyone sincere, very innocent." He paused, and then laughed somewhat self-consciously.

"But then due to certain factors some become difficult persons," the Dalai Lama continued. "But I always feel society as a whole should give some hope, some positive encouragement to those prisoners. Society rejects someone who once made some major mistake, then considers that person a hundred percent bad, a hundred percent negative. No hope, only reject. I think that this is a mistake."

The Dalai Lama applies the same sentiment to everyone, whether they are prisoners or terrorists. That morning I had read a controversial interview with the Dalai Lama in *The New York Times*. The headline was "Dalai Lama Says Terror May Need a Violent Reply." Unfortunately, it gave readers the impression that he endorsed violence as a means to confront terrorism. His representative in New York told me that the Dalai Lama had been dismayed by the article.

Apparently, the Dalai Lama had not suggested that terror should be deterred with violence. He had simply said that the real antidote to terrorism, in the long run, is an equal mix of compassion and dialogue. He told the interviewer that it is essential to be empathic, to have an open mind, even when dealing with terrorists.

"I think all our great masters in the past, Jesus Christ, Buddha, they all emphasize working for and caring for people who are in such unfortunate situations," the Dalai Lama said to the ex-prisoners. "They believe there is potential in bad persons. They are same human beings like ourselves."

The Dalai Lama turned to Jinpa, who elaborated: "In the Buddhist scripture there is a story of a murderer, Angulimala, who killed 999 individuals and was looking for one more. His goal was to create a garland made up of 1,000 little right-hand fingers. The Buddha approached the murderer and with wisdom and compassion was able to convince him to change his evil ways. Angulimala was transformed and eventually achieved a high level of spiritual realization."

The Dalai Lama interrupted, "Buddha took on that person." He laughed at the image he had conjured up. "He used a humanly approach. The Buddha believes that there is potential in everyone, even a murderer. We are all same human being."

"There's a lot of transference of pain," Santana said to the Dalai Lama. "Society is not happy. People, they work but the work is lacking in love. They get angry when they can't get people to do what they want them to do, be the way they want them to be. They don't have the skills, like you just said; the Buddha's skillful. They don't have the skills. Or they don't have the patience or talent. Or they're just full of pain themselves. So instead of helping people, what they do is pass on this pain, this fear, this darkness. How can we get around that part?"

"But change society attitude is not easy, it takes time," the Dalai Lama said. "People like yourself, who are concerned, should have deeper awareness about nature of human mind and should not give up hope—in spite of some obstacles or painful experiences. You should keep self-confidence. That's most important. Now, my own case I lost my freedom at age sixteen, then by age twenty-four, I lost my own country. Now sixty-eight, still future uncertain. Always lots of painful news. But I never give up hope. And not only me, I think almost all Tibetan people. When we first become refugees we did not expect, we never imagine, after forty-four years still this kind of painful situation. But we keep our determination, we keep on. Truth is its own strength. Initially may not obvious. But then time passes, strength grows, and grows, and grows."

He looked around the room and saw that the actor Richard Gere, dressed in a suit and tie, was standing to the side, behind a cameraman.

"Richard Gere told me about Kiran Bedi," the Dalai Lama continued. "And also I know her. I met her several times. She really carries something like new experiment in Tihar, Delhi. Her initiative I think really makes big difference. That means, yes, there is basis to change, to give hope. Possible to increase hope, increase self-confidence."

In 1972, Kiran Bedi was the first woman to be accepted into the Indian Police Service, and in time, came to be its highest-ranking female officer. Some years later, she became a household name when she had the audacity to order the towing of Prime Minister Indira Gandhi's car, which had been parked illegally.

By the early 1990s, she had quickly risen through the ranks to become the inspector general of Delhi's Tihar Prison, one of the largest in Asia with nearly ten thousand inmates. The prison's conditions were bleak: overcrowding, abysmal sanitation, and rampant violence. The motto of the jail staff was: Oppress, deprive, isolate, and punish. It was a notorious "hellhole of crime."

From the beginning of her new appointment, Bedi wanted to turn the prison into a spiritual retreat. She was convinced that prisons should rehabilitate and not punish.

In early 1994, Bedi organized a silent retreat for more than a thousand inmates. It was the largest meditation course ever held in modern times, inside or outside of prison walls. Participants spent a rigorous ten days learning Vipassana, an ancient Buddhist meditation technique that is similar to Zen meditation. Talking, reading, drinking, smoking, and sexual activity were forbidden. Meals, rest times, and periods of meditation were strictly scheduled. No one was allowed to leave once the course had begun.

During the retreat, the prisoners focused on their breathing and became more aware of the natural rhythm of their physical sensations, the way that thoughts came and went. Then the mind began to quiet down, allowing a process of self-examination. Anger and the desire to commit crimes were reduced. So was the desire for revenge.

The retreat was so successful that the government of India created the first permanent center for the practice of meditation in prison, and decided that meditation courses should be introduced in all the prisons in the country.

Bedi received the Ramon Magsaysay Award—the Asian equivalent of the Nobel Prize—for her work in Tihar.

Luz Santana, the first speaker, was a middle-aged Latina woman with short, well-coiffed brown hair. At the end of the row sat a Native American man in a bright yellow T-shirt inscribed with the word NATIVE. A flamboyant purple headscarf covered his shaved head, pirate style. Then there was the distinguished-looking man in an immaculate Zen robe. He wore it over a dark business suit and pearl-colored tie. I could imagine Central Casting easily finding him a role as a successful middle-aged CEO in a Hollywood film.

His name was Fleet Maull. He adjusted his lapel mike and looked expectantly at the Dalai Lama.

When there was a lull in the conversation, he addressed the Tibetan leader, "Your Holiness, the prison world is one of anger. That's the world you live in. The anger builds and builds and builds. It becomes your life. Male prisons are very dangerous, very violent places. You have a good chance of getting raped. You might even have to make a decision, either to be raped or to kill someone to keep from getting raped. Or join a gang that will protect you. But then that gang may require you to kill other people. So people find themselves in situations where they just have to survive. I've spent fourteen years in a federal maximum-security prison hospital, so I know."

The Dalai Lama listened intently, nodding from time to time. His lips were tense and unusually pursed together. His face was angled slightly downward, but his eyes never left Maull's face.

He was clearly weighed down by the enormity of what he was hearing.

"Because I was in a federal prison hospital, I learned that men were dying there of AIDS and other diseases. So we started this hospice in a prison, a program to care for dying men," Maull said.

The Dalai Lama took a long, deep breath and exhaled audibly.

"I was very lucky I had a meditation practice so I could keep my peace of mind, keep my heart open. I could work with my mind and try to be of service. So I did that for eleven years in prison—meditating and doing my hospice work. So, Your Holiness, it's possible to turn your time in prison into a healing journey, a transformative journey as well as a path of service."

In the late 1970s, Fleet Maull had gotten an M.A. in contemplative psychology from Naropa University and then started to study Tibetan Buddhism in Colorado with Chögyam Trungpa, one of the most influential Tibetan teachers in the West. Maull also had a secret life. He was heavily into drugs and alcohol and sporadically smuggled cocaine from Bolivia into the United States. In the mid-1980s, he was convicted of cocaine trafficking and sentenced to a prison term of twenty-five years without parole.

For Maull, the first few months in prison were a hellish descent into fear, darkness, and depression. He was devastated by what he had done to his life, by his abandonment of his young son.

Meditation became his lifeline. He knew that to survive, to hold on to his sanity, he had to pursue it with great seriousness. He began to sit for two, three, then four hours a day.

Then he had an experience that proved pivotal. He was meditating one night and suddenly noticed that his mind was totally still, impeccably focused. He was aware of all the noise and commotion surrounding him, but he wasn't distracted by any of it. He'd had many experiences like this in intensive meditation retreats, but never in the midst of such chaos. Maull saw for the first time that this could be workable.

Even though he continued to experience moments of great sadness and pain, his meditation sustained him.

"When we have a practice, it works, we survive," Fleet Maull said to the Dalai Lama. "However, for most prisoners, they don't have the tools. Tools like meditation could help them survive with their hearts open—rather than survive by becoming tough and violent and angry."

The Dalai Lama turned to Jinpa and spoke to him in Tibetan.

Jinpa translated, "His Holiness said that he is delighted with your change of heart. He said that your transformation in prison, when you were confronted by such a difficult situation, should serve as an inspirational model to many people."

I sensed that the Dalai Lama's meeting with the prisoners affected him deeply. He has heard many stories about abysmal conditions in prisons from Tibetan refugees who have spent time in Chinese *laogais*, but this was the first time he had heard that there are 6 million inmates locked up in American prisons and that so many of them are trapped in a world of anger and despair. He was saddened by this knowledge. And his heart went out to those who have lost their freedom.

TO KILL A STRANGER

Workman Avenue winds through an unremarkable residential section of West Belfast, Northern Ireland. Three-story brick houses line both sides of the narrow street, and gently rolling hills can be seen in the near distance. The most noticeable feature of the neighborhood is the imposing six-meter-high steel gate that barricades the street, preventing through traffic for both pedestrians and motor vehicles. It is one small section of the notorious Peace Line, several miles of discontinuous barriers that for the past four decades have divided the Catholic Falls district from the Protestant Shankill district west of downtown Belfast. It was the scene of devastating confrontations, untold numbers of shootings and bombings—a grim reminder and consequence of the communities' tragic failure to live together.

On this sunny fall day in October 2000, the temperature was pleasant and the sky was impossibly blue, disrupted only by a few wispy clouds. Despite the ominous presence of the barricade, the mood on both sides of the divide was festive. A large group of students in school uniforms chatted loudly on the Protestant side. Next to them were about a dozen men with television cameras. A girl in her twenties carried a large hand-drawn sign: LONG LIVE THE DALAI LAMA AND FREE TIBET. Several constables, looking sharp in white shirts and black ties, stared at the unusual sight of prayer flags strung overhead across the width of the narrow street.

A small convoy of cars, preceded by a six-man police motorcycle escort, pulled up near the gate. The Dalai Lama, with the help of a tall police officer in a dark suit, emerged from a fire-engine red compact.

He was greeted by Reverend Barry Dodds, a Protestant minister, and Father Gerry Reynolds, a Catholic priest, both involved in Catholic-Protestant reconciliation. Both men, in their eagerness, addressed him at once.

The Dalai Lama smiled, but he had trouble understanding what they said. A sizable crowd had gathered, the noise level was high, and the Irish accents unfamiliar. The two men, in their dark suits and clerical collars, looked remarkably alike—both wore large glasses, and both had mustaches and luxuriant beards.

Reynolds said to the Dalai Lama, "We are from both sides of the wall." And Dodds explained, "We are Protestant and Catholic. We will be walking with you."

The Dalai Lama finally realized that the two men came from different Christian traditions, that they were religious leaders of the two warring factions in Northern Ireland. He grabbed them by their necks and pulled them close in a fierce bear hug. And he held them thus, their cheeks pressing tightly against his own, for a long moment.

The occasion held great significance for the Dalai Lama. He religiously followed world affairs on the shortwave radio in his meditation room at home in Dharamsala. He had listened to numerous reports on the sectarian conflict, courtesy of the BBC World Service. Now, on his first visit to Northern Ireland, he had been whisked to the epicenter of the Troubles as soon as his plane touched down at Belfast International. He could see the heavy steel-and-concrete fortification of this section of the Peace Line, a physical structure designed to keep the Catholics and the Protestants from each other's throats. The gates of the barricade, locked most days of the year, would open momentarily. And the Dalai Lama, in a gesture heavy with symbolism, would cross the divide.

As the Dalai Lama started to walk, men with television cameras and long boom microphones jockeyed for positions. Security personnel, both Tibetan and Irish, tried in vain to keep the crowd from pushing closer. The Dalai Lama threaded his arms from back to front through the crooks of the elbows of the two Christian clerics so that his hands grasped theirs in a handshake slightly ahead of their bodies. He stopped by a group of schoolboys standing on the curb. They were turned out in dark blue blazers with charcoal-gray pants. Their school ties were a little askew, but their white shirts were carefully starched and ironed.

The Dalai Lama let go of the hands of the two clerics, walked up to one boy, shook his hand and stroked his hair. Next in line was a boy with very pronounced buck teeth. When the Tibetan grabbed his hands, he screamed with pleasure, as if he had met a rock star. An older girl stepped off the curb to take a picture. There was much laughter. Then the Dalai Lama decided that he wanted a group photo. He beckoned to a boy who obediently came to stand beside him. He waved a few more over, draping each arm around a pair of skinny shoulders. Flashes went off and camera shutters clicked as photographers made the most of this impromptu photo op. The Dalai Lama kissed the cheek of the boy closest to him and continued his walk toward the huge steel gates.

Two men in suits swung the heavy gates open and the Dalai Lama, his palms pressed together in front of his face, slowly walked through the gates into the Catholic enclave. There was a deafening cheer from the children on both sides. He raised his palms above his head in greeting as vivid rows of flags fluttered around him, Irish ones on Catholic turf, British ones on the Protestant side, all mingled with those decorated with Buddhist and Christian images and inscribed with prayers written by schoolchildren. The Dalai Lama stopped a short distance beyond the gates to lead a minute of silence.

After his walk through the Peace Line gates with the two religious leaders, the Dalai Lama gave an open-air address nearby. Directly behind him was the backdrop of the large brick-and-steel gates, topped with razor wire, of the Lanark Way Peace Line. Adjoining the gates were rows of high walls and a fenced-off no-man's-land. One long street was entirely devoid of any signs of life, cordoned off by railings on one side and a high wall on the other. Protestant Loyalists had been known to regularly cross over to the Catholic Falls, start a fight, and then speed home along Lanark Way, one of the few direct routes between the two warring groups.

"Differences, differences of opinion, differences of interest always there," the Dalai Lama said. "Even with myself, morning one idea, evening another idea. These two ideas may be contradictory. As long as human beings remain on this planet, some kind of conflict always there. Everybody wants happy life, safe life. Violence is opposite of that. Violence cannot solve the problem. Once violence, then counterviolence, no end. Innocent people on the street, children, women, they suffer. Keep your determination and hope. Try to make peace with more patience. Do you think some sense? If make sense, then please implement. Then I would like to thank my Protestant and Catholic brothers. This spirit, please keep in your mind, in your community. Please, okay. Thank you."

The Dalai Lama pulled the two religious leaders together and hugged them. Then, with a mischievous glint in his eyes, he reached up and tugged at their beards.

☙

After three decades of internecine warfare, things were starting to improve in Belfast, Northern Ireland's biggest city. As I walked to City Hall, I didn't see any tanks on the street, nor did I see machine-gun-toting military personnel. Even the police were thin on the ground. Yet I had an uneasy feeling as I left the hostel, one day after the events at the Peace Line. The side streets were largely deserted, much like the ghost towns of Detroit or Atlanta's inner cities. With all shops locked up at six p.m., and pubs and cafés closed soon after, a sizable area of downtown was devoid of street action, even on weekends. After living with gratuitous violence for so long, it was not easy for the inhabitants to feel comfortable in the streets after dark.

The imposing City Hall, an architectural masterpiece, was built at great expense in the Baroque Revival style. It was constructed of gorgeous Portland stone excavated from a quarry in Devon, England. Surrounding the edifice are inviting green lawns that become packed during lunch hour, when office workers grab a quick picnic.

Inside the main hall, on a stage before a series of large stained-glass windows depicting the kings and queens who visited Belfast in the nineteenth century, the Dalai Lama held court for about three hundred people. Watching him, I had the distinct feeling that he was slightly uncomfortable sitting in the straight-backed chair with only a tiny upholstered seat. There were few overt signs, but it was clear to those of us who knew his body language that he would have preferred a large armchair where he could relax, take off his shoes, and fold his legs into a lotus.

"I'm very happy to meet you," he said to the small group of Northern Irish people seated on stage with him. "I know that you have all experienced very difficult situations. Personally, same painful experience. So good opportunity to share your feeling, your sadness."

Several of them had had firsthand, life-shattering experiences during the Troubles.

Mary Hannon-Fletcher was one of them. She sat in a wheelchair next to the Dalai Lama. She was an elegant woman of about forty, with a serene presence, and wore a well-cut black jacket over a pink blouse.

Hannon-Fletcher said in a matter-of-fact voice, "When I was young, in October 1975, I was coming home from the cinema one evening when I sensed a car slowing down beside me." She had been mildly concerned at first, but then had ignored it, as she was with a young man and they were at a pedestrian crossing. Then she saw the windows of the car winding down and guns pointing out at them. "I thought, 'My God, they are going to shoot us!'" Hannon-Fletcher said. At the back of her mind, she had half expected the young man to remind her that they had just seen *The Godfather, Part II*, and that the gangster movie was likely playing havoc with her imagination. Then the unthinkable happened.

"I remember hearing a huge explosion and I was pushed to the ground," Hannon-Fletcher continued. The Dalai Lama looked up at the ceiling, his face uncharacteristically grave. "After a few seconds the explosion stopped. I tried to get up and the boy said, 'Lie down and pretend you are dead.' And that was when I realized they were still shooting. When it all stopped, he stood up. I tried to stand as well but I couldn't. I was amazed because I hadn't felt anything."

Eventually, the ambulance arrived. It was only when the paramedics came to lift her that she realized something was terribly wrong. She began to scream in agony.

Hannon-Fletcher never walked again. She and her friend had been mistakenly fingered as belonging to a Unionist paramilitary organization and were shot by members of the IRA. She spent months at the Royal Victoria Hospital and later at rehabilitation centers, beginning life anew in a wheelchair.

"I think that no other family should have to suffer like that," she told the Dalai Lama, who was watching her closely. Her tone was even, but everyone in the audience could sense her anguish. "I don't think it is acceptable. I don't think anybody has the right to take another life or to harm someone. That would be my greatest gripe. We need decent, honest people to work hard to help us get peace, to put an end to the Troubles. And that's what I want to say."

The room erupted in applause. A man in dark glasses sitting next to Hannon-Fletcher put a hand on her shoulder and said something to her. She giggled demurely, her face glowing from the effort of controlling her emotions.

The centuries-old enmity between the Protestants and the Catholics baffled the Dalai Lama. During an earlier address at the City Hall, he had told a youthful audience, "In a way, isn't it incredible that people of the same Christian faith should fight each other? It seems foolish. If somebody compared Buddhism and Christianity, then there are big differences. But not between Protestants and Catholics. You and I have more differences than you do among yourselves. But I wish for you that you never lose hope. I can do nothing. The final outcome lies in your hands, you young people of Northern Ireland."

The Dalai Lama himself has never lost hope about Tibet.

The Chinese have now occupied Tibet for close to half a century, and the signs of Sinification are more and more pronounced. Beijing's grip on the Tibetan plateau is unrelenting and there is little progress toward resolution.

"These days the Chinese government accuse me," the Dalai Lama told the Irish victims sitting onstage with him. "They create a picture of me like semi-devil." He placed his hands on top of his head, his forefingers upright. "They call me 'monster with a human face and animal's heart,' and 'a scum of Buddhism.'" He broke up and indulged in a paroxysm of belly laughs. "And last year they created one rumor in China which also reached Lhasa. They said that the Dalai Lama already got cancer, so the Dalai Lama is cancer patient, so within few months he will die."

Looking back at many difficult years, the Dalai Lama told me that these were the times when he developed the most inner strength. He believes that his spiritual practice has matured after emerging from the crucible of great trauma. To this day, he regularly visualizes his enemies deliberately trying to make his life miserable—the better to help him cultivate a deeper pool of patience while facing adversity. He is convinced that without patience it is difficult to develop meaningful love and compassion. Even minor irritations would be distracting. If our lives were easy and lacked challenges, we would become complacent. The Dalai Lama has told me several times during our interviews that his best teachers are his enemies and that it is necessary to treat them with respect and even gratitude.

Alistair Little, a quiet and intense man, sat to the left of the Dalai Lama, directly across from Mary Hannon-Fletcher. He was in his early forties, his hair close-cropped. He wore a simple, dark blue sweater that showed off his muscular physique. He projected a quiet, powerful presence but seemed strangely subdued, as if he felt out of place. After Hannon-Fletcher settled back into her wheelchair, Little addressed the Dalai Lama.

"My first contact with the conflict of Northern Ireland was when I was fourteen," Alistair Little said, his eyes directed at the floor. "My hometown had been destroyed twice by IRA bombs. The father of a friend I went to school with was killed by Catholic Republican gunmen. There was a sense of growing up losing all that was dear to you. I joined the paramilitary at age fourteen and, at the age of seventeen, went to prison and served thirteen years."

Little had joined the radical Ulster Volunteer Force after he saw the coffin of his friend's father draped in the Union Jack. He was especially devastated when he saw the man's young daughter. She had been shot in the legs when the IRA guerrillas opened fire on her father. Little vowed that if he ever had the opportunity to retaliate, he would.

Three years later, Little went to a terraced home in Lurgan, County Armagh, fired his gun through the front window, and killed nineteen-year-old Jim Griffin, a Catholic. Apparently, Griffin had made threats to some of his Protestant coworkers. Eleven-year-old Joe Griffin watched his brother die from a few feet away. Little later said that if he had known that the boy was the brother, he would have killed him, too. He harbored such a rage at the time that he thought he could even get on a bus and kill everyone.

The Dalai Lama shook his head gently, taken aback by meeting someone who was capable of killing a stranger in anger. He knows that anger and hatred warp our perspective, so that all negative aspects of our alleged antagonist are hugely exaggerated.

"While in prison, I had already begun a journey of reflection," Little continued with his story. "For about two years I reflected upon the use of violence, upon my role within the conflict. I constantly felt guilty about the pain that I caused my family. Both my parents had aged ten years in a matter of months."

Little stopped speaking. He stared at his microphone as if it were an object of infinite fascination.

Little finally regained his composure and continued in a strained voice, "For the first time, I was able to see my enemies as human. Before that I had them demonized and it's easy to commit acts of violence on someone whom you have demonized. You don't consider their pain, you don't consider their families, and you don't consider the damage you are doing to yourself. On my release from prison, I wanted to redeem myself by working for the community, helping those who were scarred by the violence. But I am unable to find inner peace. I think that is the price you pay for being involved in violence."

At this point, the man in tinted glasses sitting next to Mary Hannon-Fletcher raised his hand and the Dalai Lama looked at him expectantly.

A PASSING CLOUD

"My name is Richard Moore. I met the Dalai Lama yesterday," the man in tinted glasses said to the crowd. "I feel as if we're old friends now. At least that's what I'm telling everybody back in Derry."

In an instant, the atmosphere in the main hall of the Belfast City Hall changed. Alistair Little's story about his killing and his subsequent transformation in prison had brought tears to many. It had been difficult to watch the ex-paramilitary, who sat slouched in his chair with his eyes downcast. An unrelenting melancholy clung to him. He seemed immersed in his own tragic universe, reliving the horrors of guns, death, and long stretches of ennui while incarcerated.

Moore, however, was upbeat, irreverent, and remarkably relaxed. He was in his late thirties, well groomed, and he wore a spiffy brown suit set off by a striped purple tie. Mary Hannon-Fletcher turned around in her chair to look at him with a smile.

"As you know, I'm blind," Moore said. "I explained that to the Dalai Lama. And of course he talked about how much better I can see. That I have better focus and things like that."

That Moore was blind was not obvious. The lenses of his glasses were light brown and I could easily see through them. He did not have a cane with him. Someone had held him by the elbow and helped him mount the stage. For a blind man, he seemed inordinately at ease with his surroundings.

"So I suggested to the Dalai Lama," Moore continued after a well-timed pause, "that he should come to my home and tell that to my wife." Another theatrical pause. "He didn't."

The heavy sense of tragedy and foreboding had dissipated. Laughter now rang throughout the room. The Dalai Lama was smiling, too.

❧

The bonding between the Dalai Lama and Richard Moore had started a day earlier in Derry. They and six others had been sitting at a table having lunch in a gorgeous, light-filled room.

Moore happened to sit next to the Tibetan leader, who took a fork and, carefully using both hands, placed it into the blind man's hand.

"I'm hungry now," Moore said.

"Me, too. Some rice?" the Dalai Lama said. Without waiting for a reply, he proceeded to heap rice, one full scoop after another, onto Moore's plate.

Father Laurence, the Benedictine monk who had invited the

Dalai Lama to Northern Ireland, was curious about Moore's blindness. "What exactly do you see?" he asked.

"I don't see blackness," Moore replied. "I see everything that is happening here. I see everyone in the room, the tables, and all sitting here. The main outlines are all there as I imagine them."

"Do you see features, what features do you see? Can you describe His Holiness?" Father Laurence asked.

"Oh God, no, he is a friend of mine, I don't want to destroy that," Moore said in mock horror.

The Dalai Lama had just eaten a large French fry. He put down his fork and took off his glasses. "I think you can check. My face. Go ahead," he said, grabbing Moore's hands and placing them on his face.

"Oh, you are very good-looking," Moore said, rubbing the Dalai Lama's cheeks with his hands.

"Then nose, nose," the Dalai Lama urged him.

"Big nose." Moore pinched the nose. The Dalai Lama, sans glasses, threw his head back and laughed uproariously. He seemed to think it hilarious to have someone he barely knew rubbing his hands over his face and joking about his features.

"My hair," the Dalai Lama commanded, his playful side in full bloom. Moore obligingly put his hand on the closely shaved crown and rubbed. "Very thick hair, very thick hair," he said.

The Dalai Lama put his glasses back on. "Usually wear glasses," he told Moore, and guided the blind man's hands onto them.

"You wear glasses," Moore, said. "That means your eyesight is slightly better than mine."

The Dalai Lama turned his full attention back to his food, too hungry to continue with the horseplay, but the uncommon chemistry between the two during this first encounter would define their relationship.

❧

Inside the City hall next day, the sun was streaming through the tall, stained-glass windows. The refracted light bathed the stage evenly, backlighting the Dalai Lama and the three victims of the Troubles.

"My story begins in 1972, when I was ten years old." Moore leaned toward Mary Hannon-Fletcher and addressed the Dalai Lama, who was seated on the far side of her. "I was on my way home from school in Derry. A British soldier fired a rubber bullet from about ten feet. I was struck here, on the bridge of the nose. My nose was flattened, one eye was torn from its socket and hanging loosely close to my cheekbone. Everything went dark."

When Moore regained consciousness, he found himself stretched out on a canteen table in the school cafeteria. His music teacher was trying to cut his school bag and bloodied shirt off him. His face was so disfigured that the teacher could not even identify Moore as one of his students.

"The next thing I remember was waking up in the ambulance and my father and my sister were beside me," Moore continued. "My father was holding my hand, and he said, 'Richard, you'll be okay.' My mother was outside the ambulance and they wouldn't let her in; she was too upset. I spent two weeks in the hospital. At first, they thought that I might die from the injuries. Then they thought that I might have had brain damage. The final thing was my eyesight."

The audience was engrossed by the account. A young girl held her palms to her cheeks, a study in concentration. A few elderly women in the front rows had their eyes closed, seemingly in meditation.

"When I got out of the hospital," Moore said. "my brother would take me for a walk up and down a small garden every day. On this particular day, he said, 'Richard, do you know what happened?' And I said yes, I knew I was shot. He said, 'Do you know what damage was done?' And I said no. And he told me that I had lost this eye and I would never be able to see with the other one again. And I accepted it just like that."

Moore snapped his fingers, the sound piercing the unnatural stillness of the room.

"That night I cried when I was in bed on my own," Moore continued. "I cried for the first time. And I cried because I realized that I was never going to see my mother and my father's faces again. When you're a young boy, you don't think about getting a job, you don't think about education. You don't think about what you're going to do with the rest of your life. I just felt that I would never see my mammy and my father again. And I cried myself to sleep."

Seven years after the Belfast meeting with the victims of the Troubles, Moore invited the Dalai Lama to Derry in 2007 as a guest of honor and keynote speaker at a conference focusing on the rights of children. He sent me an invitation as well.

A few days before the Dalai Lama arrived, Moore opened his home to my family. During that year, my elder daughter, Lina, then thirteen, directed and produced a documentary film about the sectarian strife in Northern Ireland, as part of her grade-nine curriculum. She was keen to talk to Richard Moore and his mother as part of her project.

Florrie, as Moore's mother is known, was in her early eighties. She was spry, vital, and capable of talking up a storm. She took to Lina right away and was eager to share her reminiscences about her son and the tragic events of 1972.

She told us that 1972 had been a terrible year in Derry. There was constant violence on the streets, and the family was under a great deal of pressure. Her brother, Gerald McKinney, had been shot five months earlier, during the infamous Bloody Sunday, January 30, when, in less than an hour, fourteen unarmed Catholic demonstrators had been killed by soldiers of the British Parachute Regiment. It was an event that changed the history of the struggle in Northern Ireland. The outrage and unrelenting violence that followed ended an essentially nonviolent campaign for civil rights. The Troubles, a civil war that defined Northern Ireland for three decades and was responsible for 3,700 deaths, was about to see the worst violence of a long struggle.

The death of Moore's uncle Gerald was closely followed by the shooting that cost him his eyesight. The two events nearly destroyed the family.

"I lost my memory," Florrie Moore told us. "Would you believe it? There are things I can't remember when Richard was hit. Everything was a blank to me. I couldn't eat, nor sleep, and I didn't want him to know that, that I was worried about him. But it's just . . . you couldn't help it. I wondered what he was going to do and what was for him in life. It was just awful."

"I can remember lying in my bed at night awake," added Moore, sitting on a couch next to his mother. "She didn't realize that I was awake and she was beside my bed. She was literally brokenhearted and praying to God. I remember her saying, 'He is only a ten-year-old boy, please give him his eyesight back.' She was desperate. I'm told that my father stood in the street and cried, but I don't think I'd ever seen my daddy cry."

"Liam kept it all in," Florence Moore said. "I could cry but he couldn't. I think it had done him more harm. Richard was his whole world. I think if he was alive today, he'd be very happy to see how Richard has got on and his raising a family and all. I think he would be very happy."

While Richard lay unconscious in the hospital, Liam Moore had tracked down the emergency room doctor and asked, "Can I give my son my eyes?" He had been ready to sacrifice his own sight so that his ten-year-old son would be able to see. It was only after his father's death that Richard Moore learned about this act of generosity.

❧

Before the conference in Derry officially started, Moore and the Dalai Lama spent a morning fielding questions from the press. Lina was excited. She had received an official media badge from the organizers earlier, and this would be her first press conference. She made certain that she had plenty of mini tapes and spare batteries for her camcorder. She was sitting on the floor, bracing the camera on her knees, when the Dalai Lama and Moore entered the room.

Moore has been a celebrity in Derry and his story was widely known locally. But the Dalai Lama wanted the world to learn about him; he was eager for the international journalists to hear the story of forgiveness.

"Richard Moore, he is always calm, happy, and full of spirit," he told the assembled reporters and TV crews. "He was shot when very small, now cannot see. I doubt if the same sort of tragedy happen to me, whether I act like him or not. I don't know. In his case, he actually experimented. He practiced forgiveness. In my case, not yet experimented."

I had some trouble understanding what he meant with the word "experimented." I guessed the Dalai Lama wanted to say that while he has often talked about forgiveness, he himself has not experienced such a life-changing trauma. He couldn't be sure that, if he were in Moore's shoes, he could summon up the wherewithal to forgive the perpetrator so readily.

The Dalai Lama turned to look at Moore and said, "I asked

him what kind of relationship with his mother. He told me very warm, very close feeling. I think that's one major factor he becoming more compassionate person. When that unexpected tragedy happened, his response more calm. Not anger, not hatred."

Moore has never allowed bitterness to stunt his positive attitude to life. "I learned to see life in a different way," he said, describing his remarkable acceptance of what, for most, would be a debilitating trauma. "My daddy always said, 'Never let a passing cloud ruin a sunny day.'"

"There were a couple of reasons why I accepted being blind so quickly," Moore said. "I had a lot of immediate support from family and friends. There was a lot of attention from the local and national media. Political leaders came to my house and fussed over me. Overnight I was a celebrity and I was made to feel important. Another thing: I was born a happy kid. I was given a happy, contented disposition. I got that from my parents. I never heard them say an angry word, not once."

Moore and the Dalai Lama were sitting next to each other on the small stage, holding hands. The Tibetan leader did not relinquish his grip even when he leaned forward to emphasize a point.

"And when I first met him," the Dalai Lama continued, "he told me that after his eyesight lost, now feeling no more opportunity seeing his mother's face. Very touching. This shows his very close feeling with his mother. This also demonstrates his strong sense of human affection, which he got from his mother."

The Dalai Lama turned and looked at Moore again. He let go of the blind man's hand, stood up, and moved his chair closer to his. Then he reached out and grabbed his hand again.

"So now I want to tell you," he continued. "This morning his wife and two daughters come together to see me. So I tease him. Because of his peace of mind he met beautiful wife. He cannot see the face of the wife. But I can see. Very beautiful. And his two daughters, very attractive. He cannot enjoy that. But I can."

The room erupted in laughter. "So therefore I told his daughters," the Dalai Lama said, "that they should carry their father's spirit, his practice of forgiveness on the basis of compassion. Not only for their generation but also next generation. Their children and their children's children should carry their father's, their grandfather's spirit. I express to them this morning like that. Richard Moore is my hero. Whether he believes it or not, I don't know."

Moore replied instantly, "If you say it, I believe it."

A GIFT FOR
THE DALAI LAMA

Richard Moore's organization, Children in Crossfire, was founded in 1996 and has done much to raise awareness about the plight of poor children in fourteen countries, including Brazil, Colombia, Malawi, Gambia, Guinea, Ethiopia, and Bangladesh. Children in Crossfire has initiated projects ranging from working with street kids and rehabilitating child soldiers to creating agriculture and water system programs. On the afternoon before the Dalai Lama was scheduled to arrive in Derry, Moore had invited my daughter Lina and me to the organization's office in Derry. He recounted the story of his shooting and showed us the rubber bullet that blinded him.

"A lot of people think a rubber bullet is a small pellet," Moore said, holding the black projectile in his hand. It was made of hard rubber, about seven inches long, with a diameter of an inch or so. "It travels at a hundred miles an hour. It came from this side and hit me on the bridge of the nose here. You can see the damage it can cause. It's not very flexible." I could well imagine the devastation it had done to a boy of ten when it was fired from a distance of ten feet.

Moore was surprisingly relaxed, considering that the international conference he was organizing was about to begin. And the guest of honor, the Dalai Lama, was due to arrive the next day.

Moore wanted to tell us what had happened after the emotionally charged meeting with the victims of the Troubles during the Dalai Lama's first trip to Northern Ireland in 2000. The Dalai Lama had returned to Belfast in 2005 to give another lecture at the Waterfront Hall. Moore was sitting in the audience when the Tibetan leader told the crowd that the highlight of his previous visit to Northern Ireland was meeting a man from Derry who had been shot and blinded but who had, in a very short time, forgiven the man who had changed his life.

"I sat there thinking, 'That's me he is talking about.' I wanted to jump up and down and shout, 'I'm here, Your Holiness, I'm here,'" Moore said. "Of course he had no idea I was in the audience. I found the whole experience very moving."

During the drive back to Derry, Moore had an epiphany. He was touched that his story had made such an impression on the Dalai Lama. He told me, "If a great global icon like His Holiness could remember me after all these years, and thinks my story is worth telling, surely I could take the first step and try to find the man who shot me."

Over the years, Moore had repeatedly turned his thoughts to the soldier. He didn't know his name, he didn't know if he had a family or kids. He was curious to know how the man felt about firing the rubber bullet, whether he questioned the horrendous act, and whether he felt any remorse. As time went on, especially during the anniversaries of the shooting, the idea of coming face-to-face with the soldier became more urgent.

Soon after the Dalai Lama's 2005 visit to Belfast, the BBC commissioned a documentary about Moore, and in the process managed to identify and locate the soldier. Their first encounter was to be used as a key element of the film. Although Moore was keenly interested in meeting the soldier, he vetoed the idea. "I refused to let that happen for two reasons. First, I didn't want the soldier to think I was doing this for publicity reasons. And second, things change once you put a camera in the room. I didn't think the soldier could be himself and that I could be myself."

After spending several weeks agonizing over the best course of action, Moore wrote to Charles Inness, the man who blinded him: "I realize that this letter may come as a shock to you. I would like to reassure you that it is not my aim or motive to make you feel bad or guilty in any way. . . . So, why do I want to meet you? I can answer that question but not entirely. From the day I was shot I can honestly say that I have never felt a moment's bitterness towards you. As I am sure you can appreciate, the most significant thing to happen to me in my life is being shot and blinded. There was only one other person directly involved that day and that's you. I would therefore like to meet you in order to complete that circle."

It took three weeks for Inness, who lived in a small town in Scotland, to come to terms with this unexpected turn of events.

He finally wrote back to Moore and suggested that they meet in a hotel in Edinburgh.

Moore told me he had arrived early for the rendezvous. He had a drink and called his mother, who had been anxious about the meeting. He managed to reassure her. Moore then listened to his audiobook, the Dalai Lama's *Freedom in Exile*, but he couldn't concentrate.

Finally he heard footsteps approach and a mature, cultured British voice said, "Hello Richard. It's Charles Inness." Moore stood up to shake his hand and said, "Hello Charles. Good to meet you. Thanks very much for coming to see me." The thirty-three-year wait was over.

In 2007, Moore had invited the Dalai Lama to Derry to help celebrate Children in Crossfire's tenth-anniversary conference. But he struggled with one vexing question: What thank-you gift could he possibly give to the Dalai Lama?

"He is simply not into material things," he told me. "Then I thought: The best gift I could give him was the soldier. Me and the soldier. The Dalai Lama, he is the custodian of forgiveness. I thought he would appreciate meeting myself and the man who blinded me, together."

On July 17, just before the conference started, the Dalai Lama met privately with Moore and the soldier. A large contingent of international media had arrived to cover the Dalai Lama's visit to Derry. It had become known that Inness was in town, and journalists clamored to interview him. In the end it was my daughter, Lina, the enterprising thirteen-year-old filmmaker, who managed to buttonhole the soldier in the hotel corridor. Against all odds, she was the only person who succeeded in interviewing him, and I was allowed to tag along.

Inness sat across from us in his hotel room. He was in his early sixties. The years had been kind to him. Although his hair was silvery and thinning, he looked youthful and vigorous; his face, distinguished by a prominent nose, was virtually unlined and shone with good health.

Inness seemed eager to talk to us. Richard Moore is a celebrity in Northern Ireland and he has told his story many times. But so far, no one had heard directly from the soldier. Lina asked him about his meeting with Moore in Edinburgh. "It was one of those strange situations that happen to most of us," Inness told us. "You meet somebody whom you have never met and you feel you've known them all your life. We talked about our careers, our hobbies. He was with me for five hours. We didn't stop talking, time just flew."

"What exactly happened on that day in 1972?" Lina asked.

"People were throwing rocks and bricks at us, at the soldiers," Inness said. "The only means we had of getting rid of them was to go out of our shelter and shout at them. But then somebody further up the road with a rifle and a scope would shoot you dead. Or you use the rubber-bullet gun, a smooth-bore weapon. It was basically a tube, no rifling, so, ballistically, it was totally unstable. After about fifteen to twenty yards it was utterly useless.

"If it hit somebody at about twenty yards, they would turn around and wave at you. The aim was to get the soldiers to fire these things. Kids collected them as souvenirs. We fired thousands of them and the numbers that actually caused any injuries were infinitesimally small.

"When I found out afterwards what had happened to Richard, I was totally devastated. I couldn't believe it had caused such horrific injuries. If I'd known what was to happen, I definitely wouldn't have fired. But at the time, I had a perfectly sound reason for firing it; the intention was to get those kids to go away. I've never changed my view on that.

"I didn't have any guilt. But I have enormous sadness. I've never asked for Richard's forgiveness. I don't think he's got anything to forgive me for. The fact that we became very good friends is a wonderful thing."

Lina wanted to know what it was like for him and Moore to meet the Dalai Lama that morning.

"Richard had briefed His Holiness completely," Inness said. "We walked in and the Dalai Lama threw his arms around Richard as he always does. He then came and threw his arms around me, too.

"We sat down and he said, 'Tell me your story.' And I said, 'I'll look you straight in the eye and I'll tell you this: Had I known I would injure Richard so horrifically, I can assure you, Your Holiness, that there is no way on earth I'd have fired that rubber bullet.' He said, 'Absolutely, I believe you.'"

"How was your experience with the Dalai Lama?" Lina asked.

"Being the sort of person I am, it didn't faze me in the slightest to be in the Dalai Lama's presence. It was exactly as I expected. He behaved exactly the way I'd expect him to. So did Richard. It was a joyful experience."

It was standing room only in the Millennium Forum in Derry. More than a thousand guests had gathered to hear the Dalai Lama speak at the closing of the Children in Crossfire conference. Lina, proudly wearing her media pass, was allowed in as part of the press corps.

Richard Moore introduced the Dalai Lama, who then delivered the keynote speech. Toward the end of the evening, something unexpected happened. Charles Inness walked solemnly onto the stage, making an unscripted appearance. He began to address the crowd, a slight tremor in his voice. I knew how difficult it must be for him to speak to the people of Derry. Moore, after all, is their favorite son.

Inness said, "Thirty-five years ago, I took a tragic action that resulted in Richard being blinded. I was appalled and devastated by it. I was upset for many years. Now we are the best of friends. If Richard and I can do this, there's hope for this country and everyone in it."

The Dalai Lama stood up, walked to Inness, and grabbed him in a bear hug. He then pulled Moore close to him and the three locked in embrace. The blind man, the soldier who shot him thirty-five years ago, and the Tibetan. The crowd stood up as one and the applause was heartfelt and thunderous. Many were moved to tears.

The next day, my family and I met Moore again before we left for Belfast and home. Just before we boarded our bus, he confided, "I nearly collapsed when I realized that Charles was on stage. I'd promised him that I wouldn't let the media know he was in town. I wanted to protect his privacy. I'm even more amazed that it was the Dalai Lama who secretly made it happen."

Part Two

EDUCATING THE HEART

My hope and wish is that, one day, formal education will pay attention to what I call education of the heart. Just as we take for granted the need to acquire proficiency in the basic academic subjects, I am hopeful that a time will come when we can take it for granted that children will learn, as part of their school curriculum, the indispensability of inner values such as love, compassion, justice, and forgiveness.

—His Holiness the Dalai Lama

LUCY AND TING

The Dalai Lama walked onto the stage and approached the two masters of ceremony, who stood waiting to greet him. He shook hands solemnly with Stephen Boles, an eleventh-grade student, and proceeded to do the same with Anjali Appadurai. As they shook hands, the sixteen-year-old deliberately bent forward at the waist and ever so slightly inclined her head toward the Dalai Lama, who immediately reciprocated. They bumped foreheads gently as they held hands. The Dalai Lama did a double take, took a good look at her, and chuckled.

I could see that he was surprised. It was unusual for the Dalai Lama to greet someone he has never met before in this manner. I have seen him do this forehead-to-forehead greeting, a gesture of enormous respect, with important Tibetan lamas. But this was the first time I'd seen him extend it to a high school student. Appadurai had somehow, perhaps intuitively and without premeditation, seized the moment and received a special blessing.

Four more students waited at the center of the stage. The

Dalai Lama slowly walked up to each of them, again touching his forehead to theirs. Angela Tsui, the twelfth-grader, directed the Dalai Lama and Thupten Jinpa, his translator, to their leather armchairs. She would be moderating the conversation. The Dalai Lama sat down, looked out at the audience, and beamed. There was a mischievous glint in his eyes. I had the distinct feeling that he was looking forward to the dialogue with the students.

Before the Dalai Lama came onstage, I had been apprehensive and uncertain about how things would unfold. Over the years, I had organized a number of events with the Dalai Lama. World-class thought leaders and eminent scientists had come to converse with him. But now, in September 2006 at Vancouver's Orpheum theater, was the first time all his fellow panelists would be under twenty years of age.

The Dalai Lama bent down, took off his brown oxfords, and folded his legs into the lotus position in his armchair.

Tsui, an ethnic Chinese from Vancouver, said to the Dalai Lama, "Your Holiness, we know that this is the first time you have been in Canada since you were made an honorary Canadian citizen. We would love to welcome you with a special gift." She produced a maroon visor, displaying the word CANADA, from a paper bag. "We know that you like hats."

The Dalai Lama unfolded his legs, stood up again, and took the visor.

"This is very good," he said as he sat back down. "For protection, my eyes. Practical use. Although quite tight." He moved the visor so that it perched, rather than fit snugly, on his head.

"Why is it important for you to come speak with young people on the topic of compassion?" Tsui asked the Dalai Lama. She was poised, and enunciated her words clearly and slowly. There were no signs of nervousness, despite the presence of the two thousand attendees who were following her every word in the Orpheum theater, and the millions around the world who were watching the live stream.

"Quite simple," the Dalai Lama replied. "Time always moving. From past we can learn something. But important is future—because future yet to come. Future in our hands. I think every human action is supposed to do good. But out of ignorance, and also lack of wider perspective, often our action brings bad result, with painful consequences."

The Dalai Lama has often talked about "ignorance," a concept that can be difficult to grasp. It's helpful to understand the underlying idea by replacing the word "ignorance" with simple terms such as "lack of knowledge, lack of information, lack of wisdom" and thinking of ignorant actions as "misguided," or "flawed." The Dalai Lama believes that much of our suffering is caused because we lack the requisite wisdom to interpret reality accurately. Because of this ignorance, we pursue short-lived pleasures instead of meaningful happiness. For the Dalai Lama, the only way to achieve sustained well-being and inner peace is through the cultivation of altruism, through the cultivation of love and compassion. We need better and more nuanced information about what really makes us happy, and he wanted to share that information, especially with these young people.

The Dalai Lama said to the students, "The present generation, with fuller knowledge about reality, and with wider perspective, can act to bring better world, better future." He was sitting comfortably in his chair, as if he were lounging in someone's living room and had all the time in the world to examine the critical issues of the day.

"I think the elder generation, like myself who belongs to twentieth century, now we are ready to say good-bye." He rested an elbow on the armrest and delicately fluttered the fingers of his right hand in a wave, for emphasis. "My generation, who creates lot of problem on this planet, now responsibility give to young people."

He laughed as he looked at each student in turn.

"So you have to handle. This is first reason. Second reason, younger people are mentally, physically still growing. So everything very fresh. I think many troubles which we are facing today is essentially man-made problems. Naturally, no human being wants more trouble, but as I mentioned earlier, out of ignorance and lack of wider perspective, we deliberately create more problem for ourselves.

"There is a gap between reality and appearance. Always this gap. Maybe I am wrong, you have to judge. But I believe that older generation has certain ideas, certain way of thinking, fixed in the brain. So with this old way of thinking, they then try to deal with new problems. But reality, however, has changed and the method of dealing with it is old-fashioned. Reality, I think in subtle way, day by day changing, always changing. But the method to deal with this new reality is still old thinking. I feel, younger generation, easier to see this new reality. Younger generation easier to change their perception. So therefore it's very,

very important that our younger generation utilize their brain clearly and through holistic way, see clearly this new reality. And most important: act. So that's why I am very happy."

The Dalai Lama's face took on an impish expression. He pointed a finger at Jinpa, his faithful translator, and said, "Instead of seeing this old person's face, much better to look at young person." He laughed heartily, swiveled his head, and took in the smiling young students seated on either side. A little concerned that Jinpa, who was only in his early forties, might take it the wrong way, he reached out and patted his shoulder.

The Dalai Lama speaks often of the gap between reality and appearance. He is one of the most admired persons on the planet but he harbors no illusions about himself. He is always examining himself unflinchingly, assessing his own strengths and weaknesses. He sees himself as a simple Buddhist monk. He tells anyone who will listen that he has no special powers, that his ability to help is limited. He says that all he is able to do is to give some advice, to share others' worries. His modus operandi is to analyze any given situation with rigor and try to see things from multiple perspectives. This fosters a sense of care, of mindfulness, in the way he thinks, the way he conducts his affairs and interacts with people.

Lucy Wang, a twelfth-grade student, took the seat next to the Dalai Lama. She told him a story about Ting, her cousin, who lives in China. Ting, although younger, had always been the more mature, decisive, and responsible one. Since she was twelve years old, Ting had taken on the responsibility of looking after her baby sister when their parents were working. The family was poor, and Ting had to drop out of school and sell ice cream to help make ends meet.

Lucy had visited Ting during her summer break. She had not seen her cousin for some time and was shocked by her appearance. Days of standing in the scorching sun selling ice cream had disfigured her face. She looked much older, her skin was dry and peeling. The two girls started to sell ice cream together. Sales were abysmal. They managed to make only twenty cents that first afternoon, and Lucy got terribly sunburned. Ting was resigned to this hardship, as she desperately wanted to save every penny to buy a beach umbrella to shelter her from the sun, and school supplies for her sister, who was starting school in the fall.

Later that summer, an old lady in the neighborhood was diagnosed with an infection that spread from her fingers all the way to her kidneys. She urgently needed expensive medical care. Ting, without hesitation, gave all her savings, about seventy dollars, to the old woman. She told Lucy that her own needs could wait, but it was life or death for the old lady. Lucy was deeply moved by her cousin's altruism, and her own perspective on life changed.

Now, she told the Dalai Lama, she wanted to devote her life to helping others. And every day she prayed that Ting could fulfill her dreams.

After she finished her story, Lucy addressed the Dalai Lama: "Your Holiness, education teaches us everything, including compassion. But I have discovered that some people, like Ting, even though they don't have much education, still have a lot of compassion. So does that mean that education is unrelated to compassion?"

The Dalai Lama conferred with Jinpa. He wanted to be sure he understood the question.

"Firstly, I admire your way of thinking and also your cousin's. Wonderful, wonderful. Sometimes I think compassionate feeling more available among the poor, the uneducated. Why? Compassion fosters positive conditions for survival. As soon as we leave our mother's womb, the feeling of intimacy is key to survival, and to the proper development of our life. Immediately after birth, the young child is like small animal. By nature, by biology, the child senses his survival depends entirely on affection. So the child seeks immediately connection with the mother. I think mother's milk is a symbol of compassion. It is not created by religion or by education, but by nature. Without compassion we can't survive. In my own case, my first lesson of the value of compassion happened during the first hour of my birth. Tremendous feeling, deep inside. I think I still feel those first traces of emotion. I am sure I will feel them till my death.

"Now, I think people like Hitler or Stalin, we think they have no mercy, no compassion. But these people, like us, also have seed of compassion from birth. Because of certain ideology, certain environment, they develop anger, hatred, fear. These emotions then become dominant and their basic human values suppressed."

The Dalai Lama had told me that during the Second Gulf War, his heart went out to Saddam Hussein. He said that former U.S. president George W. Bush's view of Hussein was unfair and limited. Bush believed him to be unrelentingly evil and sought his elimination. But for the Dalai Lama, reality was more nuanced. He believed that Hussein was not wicked from birth, that his innate sense of compassion, while buried deep, could make eventual transformation possible. If circumstances changed, he might have been a different person.

"Now, education," the Dalai Lama continued with his response to Lucy Wang. "It helps to sustain and nurture compassion. In my own case, from my childhood, I already had some sort of feeling of compassion toward others, including animals or insects. Two small insects fight. I always want to help weaker side. I feel angry toward bigger one, sometimes I do this . . ." He bent forward, peered intently at his right hand, and flicked an imaginary insect away with his fingers. Then, as if to exorcise this unexpected action of aggression, he rubbed his palms circularly together a few times. The students were delighted with the demonstration. They were having a good time and were also visibly relaxed.

"Eventually, I understand Buddhism better, and also, I had very good teacher," the Dalai Lama continued. "So, adding education to my biological seed of compassion, I see more clearly the value of compassion. And after some time, my compassion becoming less biased. It is not dependent on others' attitude. It comes not merely from biology but through education. Through training of mind, use intelligence. I understand the value of compassion. I realize the harmfulness of anger, hatred. Use education to train your mind. With practice, my own experience deepen. More unbiased compassion brings me inner peace. Result, better physical health."

According to the Dalai Lama, the sense of affection we feel for our family and close friends is biased and tinged with attachment. It changes with circumstances. Unbiased compassion, however, is based on the realization that others, even our enemies, have the right to be happy and avoid suffering, just as much as we do. This compassion extends to everyone.

"I think I also have better mental function, and at least more friends," the Dalai Lama continued. His Canada visor proved to be too tight and he pushed it farther up so it perched precariously on his shaved head. "Wherever I go, I usually receive big smiles. I think my face is nothing special, same human face. But usually more smile. How? I don't think my smile is artificial or something calculated. I give smile, I will get money or fame or something. Not like that. No calculation, just spontaneous. I always consider anyone the same. From this human flesh"—here the Dalai Lama slapped his wrist smartly—"we all have same human emotion. So, wisdom and compassion. Compassion helps the wisdom, or intelligence, become more constructive. And intelligence nurtures, sustains compassion."

For the Dalai Lama, compassion and wisdom are the fundamental building blocks of society. In our homes and in our schools, he believes, we should systematically nurture a culture of warmheartedness, a culture of kindness. They are essential elements, critical to having a happy life.

He believes it is necessary to make substantive changes in the way we educate our youth: to balance the imperatives of academic excellence with social and emotional competencies, to foster the whole and compassionate person.

The Dalai Lama might well have put it this way: Love grows brain and brain grows love.

GOD IS NOT
A CHRISTIAN

The Chan Centre for the Performing Arts at the University of British Columbia looks like a shiny cylindrical bunker that periscopes up over a small, lush forest of Austrian pines, red cedars, and rhododendrons. Its exterior is clad in pre-weather-treated zinc panels that react chimerically to the constantly changing weather patterns of Vancouver. The structure imparts a sense of melancholy as befits its location, the wet, gray, moss-ridden environment of the Pacific Northwest. Inside is another matter. It is all blond wood, architecturally exuberant, and its acoustics are celebrated as being among the best in Canada. On this spring day in 2004, in cooperation with the university, it was fitting to have the use of this hall for one of the most anticipated dialogues in the city in recent memory.

The Dalai Lama, wearing an orange visor, was on stage sitting next to Archbishop Desmond Tutu, who had just flown in from

South Africa. The Dalai Lama sat in his usual lotus position on a leather armchair that was a size too small for his folded legs. His knees stuck out a smidgen beyond the armrests.

"My main concern," he said to Tutu, "what's the best way to talk about deeper human values like love, compassion, forgiveness, these things. Not relying on God, but relying on ourselves."

Tutu was hunched forward in his chair; he was carefully examining his hands, which were resting on his lap. He was dressed in a dark suit and a striking purple shirt with a decidedly magenta hue. A large metal cross hung below the clerical collar.

The Dalai Lama said, "I myself, I'm believer, I'm Buddhist monk. So for my own improvement, I utilize as much as I can Buddhist approach. But I never touch this when I talk with others. Buddhism is my business. Not business of other people. Frankly speaking"—he stole a glance at the archbishop and declared firmly—"when you and our brothers and sisters talk about God, creator, I'm nonbeliever." He laughed, perhaps a little self-consciously.

It seemed to me that the Dalai Lama's feelings about God have changed over the years. In an early interview, when I asked him if he thought there was a God, he answered simply, "I don't know." He took the view of an agnostic: he understood that it's not possible to know one way or another whether God exists.

"In Buddhism no creator," the Dalai Lama said at the Chan Centre. "But we also accept Buddha, bodhisattvas, these higher beings. However, if we only rely on these higher beings, we would just sit there, lazy." He leaned into his chair, threw his head back, and rolled his eyes heavenward.

"Won't help, won't help. So that's my view," the Dalai Lama concluded.

Tutu crossed his arms in front of his chest. He looked pensive, deep in thought. Then a smile creased his face.

He said, "I was thinking when you were talking about God or no God, who you blame?" Tutu lifted both his legs from the floor and rocked back and forth in his chair. He was gripped in a fit of uncontrollable mirth. Perhaps it was an inside joke. If so, I didn't get it. Perhaps he meant that if there is no God, then there is no one to blame but ourselves?

Tutu stared at the Dalai Lama as his trademark giggle filled the hall. The Dalai Lama then bowed deeply in homage, his head nearly level with his folded knees. He whipped off his visor and saluted his South African friend with an exaggerated flourish. Both men seemed to derive an enormous kick out of Tutu's cryptic question.

Tutu said nothing more for the longest time. He was gathering his thoughts, preparing to expound further on the subject. Although diminutive, all of five feet and four inches, his is an imposing figure. His facial features are broad and remarkably plastic.

Before Tutu could resume, the Dalai Lama pleaded, "I think . . . maybe I interfere. May I respond, just a little, just a little?"

"Yeah, yeah, yeah," Tutu screeched in a loud, high-pitched voice that took the audience by surprise. He turned completely sideways and trained his eyes on the Dalai Lama, his face one of pure animation. The two elderly spiritual leaders, for one short, unforgettable moment, became kids again, horsing around and thoroughly enjoying each other's company. At one gathering in Oslo, after a particularly rambunctious episode, Tutu admonished the Dalai Lama in mock seriousness, "Look here—the cameras are on you, stop behaving like a naughty schoolboy. Try to behave like a holy man."

The audience at the sold-out Chan Centre was delighted with the bantering. It was heartening to see that these two global icons did not take themselves too seriously. That they could, without being the least bit self-conscious, display such childlike playfulness. The Dalai Lama was carried along by the archbishop's animal vitality, his irreverence, his lighthearted theatrics. He was so in synch with the African that he did something I have seldom seen him do before. He interrupted Tutu, with no regard for niceties or etiquette, in mid-thought.

But now that Tutu had given him permission to interrupt, the Dalai Lama turned serious. He said to the archbishop, "The problem is, if we involve religious faith, then there are many varieties and fundamental differences of views. So very complicated.

"That's why in India"—he pointed a finger at Tutu for emphasis—"when they drafted the constitution they deliberately used secular approach. Too many religions there"—he counted them out one by one with his fingers—"Hindu, Islam, Buddhism, Judaism, Sikhism, Zoroastrianism, Jainism. So many. And there are godly religions and there are godless religions. Who decides who is right?"

Now that the Dalai Lama had his say, he put his orange visor back on his bald pate.

Tutu replied, "Let me just say that one of the things we need to establish is that"—long pause—"God is not a Christian." He paused again and turned to look at the Dalai Lama with a mischievous glint in his eyes. It had the intended effect. The Tibetan leader laughed with abandon. Apparently, Tutu was not done with horsing around.

"Are you feeling better?" Tutu asked the Dalai Lama, who inclined his body far away from his friend and covered his eyes in mock surrender.

"We could go on, but . . ." Tutu turned thoughtful. He enunciated his words with great care, and paused for a long time after each phrase. He picked up the Dalai Lama's earlier thread. "The glory about God is that God is a mystery. God is actually quite incredible in many ways. But God allows us to misunderstand her"—at this, the audience went wild; the applause was loud and spontaneous—"but also to understand her."

"I've frequently said I'm glad I'm not God," Tutu continued. "But I'm also glad God is God. He can watch us speak, spread hatred, in his name. Apartheid was for a long time justified by the church. We do the same when we say all those awful things we say about gays and lesbians. We speak on behalf of a God of love.

"The God that I worship is an omnipotent God," Tutu intoned, opening his arms wide. He paused to let this sink in.

Then he said, sotto voce, "He is also incredibly, totally impotent. The God that I worship is almighty, and also incredibly weak.

"He can sit there and watch me make a wrong choice. Now, if I was God," he said as the hall burst into laughter, "and I saw, for instance, this one is going to make a choice that is going to destroy his family, I'd probably snuff him out.

"But the glory of God is actually mind-blowing. He can sit and not intervene because he has such an incredible, incredible reverence for my autonomy. He is prepared to let me go to hell. Freely. Rather than compel me to go to heaven.

"He weeps when he sees us do the things that we do to one another. But he does not send lightning bolts to destroy the ungodly. And that is fantastic. God says, 'I can't force you. I beg you, please for your own sake, make the right choice. I beg you.'

"When you do the right thing, God forgets about God's divine dignity and he rushes and embraces you. 'You came back, you came back. I love you. Oh how wonderful, you came back.'"

There was total silence in the hall. Tutu's speech was a tour de force. The audience was captivated by his malleable facial features, which could change from fiery anger to deeply felt compassion in a heartbeat. His voice scaled multiple octaves. His arms and hands were in perpetual motion. He was a showman and preacher par excellence.

Tutu took a sip of water. He was done.

On cue, Alexander Sanchez, a young man of seventeen, walked up to the stage and stood behind the podium. He was a twelfth-grade student in a local high school, and he had been selected to ask a question of the archbishop.

"First of all, I like the visor," he said to the Dalai Lama. "Orange suits you, man." The Tibetan was confused—the young man spoke a little too fast for him. His translator said, "He likes your visor."

Sanchez addressed Tutu: "In school we read books and newspapers about all the bloodshed in Africa, about the conflicts between black and white. How do you settle disputes without taking away people's free will to choose forgiveness?"

Tutu put one palm up to his ear; he, too, seemed to have difficulty following the question. The Chan Centre has great acoustics for music, but it seemed to have challenges with the spoken word. Instead of waiting for Sanchez to repeat his question, the archbishop abruptly got out of his chair and walked up to him. They shook hands. Then Tutu raised both his palms and instructed, "High five." Sanchez was delighted to oblige. He put an arm around the archbishop and repeated his question.

"I think that many times people are more moved by example," Tutu replied after going back to his chair. "Especially examples of people who, having suffered a great deal, instead of demanding the pound of flesh in retribution, have been extraordinary.

"There have been many moments in the Truth and Reconciliation Commission. A young black woman came to us and told this story: 'The police came and took me to the police station. They put me in a room, undressed me. They took my breasts and they shoved them into a drawer. And then they'd slam the drawer several times on my nipples until the white stuff ooze.'

"Now, you imagine that someone who has experienced this kind of atrocity would be bitter, would lust after revenge. But frequently people like her would say they were ready to forgive.

The perpetrators, not always but many times, would be touched by this compassion. You can't compel someone to confess and be penitent. But you see, the thing we are talking about here, it isn't something that merely goes in the head. We are touched, we are touched, in other parts of our being. In the heart, in the feeling in the tummy. And often you see people break down and cry."

Sanchez stood rock-still behind the podium. His face was devoid of expression. Then he walked slowly down the steps and left the stage without a word, stunned by the magnitude of what he had just heard.

Later that day, Tutu and the Dalai Lama came together again in a small function room at the Chan Centre. They had another opportunity to expand on their views on religion before Tutu had to leave Vancouver.

"I think generally all religious traditions have good potential to improve human condition," the Dalai Lama said to the archbishop. "However, some followers of religions, they are not very serious about one's own teaching. They—out of selfishness, money, or power—use religion for personal gain. In some cases, because they completely isolated, so no idea about other traditions, value of other traditions. So that creates religious disharmony. But I think if you make balance, I think more weight to positive side than negative. Much, much more."

"Yes, you are right," Tutu replied. "And you have to remember that religion is of itself neither good nor bad. Christianity has produced the Ku Klux Klan. Christianity has produced those who killed doctors that perform abortions. Religion is a morally neutral thing. It is what you do with it. It is like a knife, a knife is good when you use it for cutting up bread for sandwiches. A knife is bad when you stick it in somebody's gut. Religion is good when it produces a Dalai Lama, a Mother Teresa, a Martin Luther King."

"And a Bishop Tutu," the Dalai Lama interjected.

Tutu stared at him, stuck a finger at his own chest, and admonished, "I'm talking!"

The Dalai Lama leaned back in playful recoil and laughed with abandon.

"But we've got to be very careful that we don't say . . ." Tutu continued, ignoring him. But the Dalai Lama had trouble concentrating. His chest was heaving, his shoulders were jiggling with involuntary convulsions; he was having a hard time controlling his laugher. "Because there are bad Muslims, therefore Islam is a bad religion. Because there are bad Buddhists, Buddhism is bad. Just look at the Buddhist dictators in Burma," Tutu said. "We've got to say, what does your faith make you do? Make you become? I would not have survived without the faith of knowing that this is God's world and that God is in charge, that evil is not going to prevail despite all appearance to the contrary. Yes, of course, sometimes, you want to whisper in God's ear, 'God, for goodness' sake, we know that you are in charge, but why don't you make this more obvious?'"

The Dalai Lama was not laughing any longer. He nodded vigorously as Tutu finished.

A FIRESIDE CHAT

The hotel suite had a breathtaking view of Vancouver. To the west, immediately beyond the tall buildings of downtown, I could see the shimmering silver of the Burrard Inlet, a shallow-sided coastal fjord that separates the city from the precipitous North Shore Mountains. The distinctive, enormous mass of dark green in the foreground, all 1,001 acres of it, was Stanley Park, one of the most celebrated urban parks in the world. It is home to 500,000 Douglas firs, red cedars, and Sitka spruces many of them giants that began life several centuries ago.

In the suite, Rabbi Zalman Schachter-Shalomi was having an animated tête-à-tête with Shirin Ebadi, the Nobel Peace laureate from Iran. They were chatting about the differences between two Muslim sects, the Sunnis and the Wahhabis, as they waited for the Dalai Lama to arrive. The rabbi, then eighty years old, was drinking strong cappuccino from a paper cup from a café near the hotel; he would have nothing to do with the coffee served by the caterers.

Then the Dalai Lama entered the suite, followed by his translator, Thupten Jinpa. He walked up to Ebadi and grabbed her hands. He said to her with obvious warmth, "Again we meet."

The rabbi embraced the Dalai Lama in a fierce bear hug, kissed him loudly on the cheek with undisguised relish, and said, "I hope you got some rest last night." The three had been on a panel discussion a day earlier at the University of British Columbia, where the Dalai Lama first met Ebadi, a few months after she received the Nobel Peace Prize in Oslo in 2003. The Dalai Lama and the rabbi had met before in Dharamsala.

The greetings over, the Tibetan leader gestured for everyone to sit down. I noticed he had paid no attention at all to the gorgeous panorama outside the floor-to-ceiling windows. He chose a chair facing the small group and a faux fireplace, with his back to the view. Over the years, I have seldom seen him take more than a superficial interest in his surroundings.

"Your Holiness, I want to challenge you, okay?" the rabbi said to the Dalai Lama without preamble. "There is so much deep work being done on the subtle plane. Remember we talked about angels?"

"Yes, yes," the Dalai Lama said.

❧

In 1990, a year after the Dalai Lama received the Nobel Peace Prize, Reb Zalman, as the rabbi is popularly known, and a small group of influential American Jews went to Dharamsala to begin a four-day interfaith dialogue with him. The gathering was inspired in part by the growing number of Jews who have developed an extraordinary affinity with Buddhism. The group had been keen to explore similarities between Judaism and Buddhism. But the meeting was also inspired by the Dalai Lama's interest in the Jewish Diaspora. He viewed the Jews as "survival experts" who managed to maintain their cultural and religious identities through thousands of years of exile and persecution. Tibetan Buddhists, now expelled from their homeland, face the same challenge. As one rabbi told the Dalai Lama, "The Chinese came to your people as the Germans came to ours." The Tibetan leader had also wanted to learn about Jewish meditation and the Kabbalah, which has similarities with Buddhist mysticism. That had been years ago, and the Dalai Lama was always eager to see Reb Zalman and continue their conversations.

~

"When somebody is sick, there is external medicine and there is internal medicine," Reb Zalman continued with his question to the Dalai Lama in Vancouver. "I'm looking for the deep teachings that have to do with internal medicine. The stuff that will change things on the subtle plane. You have such a wonderful tradition, just as we have in the Kabbalah. I wonder if your tradition has some skillful means for doing this special inner work."

The Dalai Lama conferred briefly with Jinpa to make certain that he understood the rabbi's question.

"As believers in the tradition, we accept that some deeper values exist," the Dalai Lama finally said. "To common people, to common sense, sometimes not obvious. One example: Tibetan medicine, although the medicine comes from different plants, different minerals, each have their own unique power. That, science can prove. But then, if you harvest some plants at different times of day, big differences in their effectiveness. Size of moon—full moon or half-moon—also makes a difference. I don't know whether science can explain or not. I don't know. But difference of effect is there.

"Then another thing, Tibetan medicine produced in Tibet becoming quite popular. Among Chinese also, particularly since the SARS epidemic. When it happened, many Chinese, including some Chinese leaders, very much look for protection from Tibetan medicine. But those medicine produced in Tibet not charged by recitation of mantra. In India, same medicine, but charged by mantra. According to some experts, medicine which we produce in Dharamsala more effective."

A number of years ago, the Dalai Lama invited me into his home to spend some time with him when he woke up and began his morning routine. After he meditated for about an hour, he took me into his bathroom, where he proceeded to brush his teeth. Then he showed me his medicine cabinet. It contained a bewildering array of both Western and Tibetan medicines. The Western ones were mostly vitamins and supplements; I had no idea about the Tibetan ones.

"Do you trust Tibetan medicine more than Western medicine?" I asked the Dalai Lama then.

"In Tibetan medicine, the stomach is like soil," the Dalai Lama replied. "If soil is good, then all can grow properly. So taking care of stomach can prevent many illnesses. I believe I have more faith in Tibetan medicine, particularly in preventing the start of problems. But if something really goes wrong, some pain, Western medicine much better. Cancer, like some other illnesses, Tibetan medicine is still not very effective. But things like hepatitis B, difficult to cure in West, Tibetan medicine is effective."

Like a lot of people, Reb Zalman was intrigued by Tibetan medicine. But at the Vancouver hotel, he was more concerned with the idea of something more esoteric. "When I was in Dharamsala, I bought some medicine and it helped me," the rabbi said. "I want to get to the question of what they call energy medicine. The world needs not only the individual. The world needs energy medicine. There are conflicts in many places, and these conflicts can't be resolved by reason alone. One has to go to the spirit. I believe there are beings that want to help us make peace. But most of us don't know how to contact them. I wish that more knowledge of the higher levels would come out."

"Of course there are mysterious levels . . ." the Dalai Lama began to reply.

Jinpa poured some hot water in a cup and placed it on a glass coffee table. Realizing that it was a stretch for the Dalai Lama to reach it, Jinpa tried to pull the heavy table closer. The Dalai Lama immediately leaned out of his chair and stopped him, saying, "No, no—no need."

"Some mysterious things certainly there," the Dalai Lama continued his reply to the rabbi. "We believe that these so-called higher beings have more energy than us. At a practical level, much depend on our own effort. If our effort comes, then some of these positive energies, I think, we can connect. From the Buddhist viewpoint, these higher beings develop higher energy because of their practice of altruism. The ultimate source of energy is altruism. This energy is always ready, like electricity, we just need to be receptive."

"Often, we say, we have to do what we can do, then God helps," the rabbi said. "When I was a child, I used to be angry when people said, 'God helps those who help themselves.' But now I fully understand that if we don't take the initiative, we cannot accept the power."

"Yes, yes, exactly," the Dalai Lama said enthusiastically.

The conversation was spontaneous, unscripted, and unexpected, and I was pleased with how the meeting was unfolding. When I first had the idea of carving out some time for the Dalai Lama and his friends, I came up with some basic guidelines. The meeting would be private. No media would be allowed. And a moderator was not needed. I simply wanted them to spend some quality time, to hang out, without the constraint of an agenda.

"There is a question here, Your Holiness," Ebadi's translator said to the Dalai Lama.

"Yes, yes," the Dalai Lama said.

"When our earthly being comes to an end, death, what happens to the energy that is stored in us?" Ebadi asked through her translator.

The Dalai Lama replied, "Now, for almost three thousand years, many people, many thinkers, investigate about it, talk about it, so different explanations, different theories. One group accepts the idea of reincarnation, life after life. For Christianity,

Muslim also I think, after death comes some period of rest, then final judgment. Although after this, the soul still remains, but there is no cycle of rebirth. If you ask me what explanation Buddhism? Then I will say: life after life. This physical body, together with our grosser mind, cease to exist. But our main mind, this means our more subtle mind, will continue. Another life begins."

The Dalai Lama was one of sixteen siblings. Many of them died soon after birth; only seven survived. After his younger sister was born, his mother gave birth to a baby boy. The family was devastated when he died two years later. It was the custom to consult lamas and astrologers before the child was buried. The family was told that he would be reborn under the same roof. A small mark was then made on the body with butter. After some time another boy was born. This turned out to be the last of the family, the youngest brother of the Dalai Lama. Sure enough, the family could make out a pale mark, on exactly the same spot where the butter had been smeared. The Dalai Lama said he had no doubt that the two boys were the same being, given another chance to begin life once again.

"How long until when, what happens when this other life gets released and continues?" Ebadi went on with this train of thought.

"Until what we Buddhists call final salvation—'salvation' means we are free, liberated, achieved nirvana—mind has no end," the Dalai Lama replied. "We become higher being. Then we have more responsibility to help others." He sat back in his chair and had a good laugh. His funny bone was tickled by the idea that just when we would be finally able to retire for good, after untold lifetimes of performing good deeds, more responsibility would be waiting.

The Dalai Lama took a long drink of hot water and stared unwaveringly at Ebadi.

"Now I would like to ask you a question," he said to her.

He put the cup down and leaned forward in his chair.

"Firstly, I admire your work. The change in your country, by your own people, from within," he spoke in a deliberate manner. He paused carefully after each sentence, making sure to give the translator sufficient time.

He said, "As a Muslim country, and according to Koran, that's wonderful. At the same time lots of obstacles. Some of these obstacles may not be bad intention, but I think narrow-mindedness. Importance is educate these people through media. But media censorship is another obstacle. So your position not easy. My question is . . ."

He switched to Tibetan, and Jinpa translated, "You have a difficult situation. Would it help your cause if a gathering of Nobel laureates could be arranged in Iran? Would their presence help?"

The Dalai Lama interjected at length in Tibetan before Ebadi could reply.

"Of course this is not to say that His Holiness would like to come," Jinpa translated. "But His Holiness has been feeling strongly that the Nobel Peace laureates should take a more active role in conflict resolutions. Especially in preventative measures in areas where there is potential for major conflicts. His Holiness has spoken quite extensively with President Havel of the Czech

Republic. Havel has a nonprofit foundation called Forum 2000, and he is thinking about bringing this initiative under that umbrella. Elie Wiesel is interested as well."

"If such a gathering happens in Iran, it would be extremely beneficial," Ebadi replied through her translator. "However, I don't think the present government would like to see it happen. They are immensely afraid of any discussion of democracy and rights."

I could sense a great deal of warmth and respect between the two Nobel Peace laureates. Since they had met for the first time a day earlier, I noticed that the Dalai Lama made a point of connecting with Ebadi at every opportunity. They have much in common: religion in their genetic makeup, an über-rational worldview, a passion to help the oppressed. There are a few other laureates with whom the Dalai Lama has great personal chemistry—Archbishop Desmond Tutu, for instance. I felt privileged to be present at the beginning of this bond between the Buddhist and the Muslim.

The Dalai Lama has made a lot of effort to reach out to Muslims in the last few decades and has participated in numerous interfaith gatherings. I know that he rejoiced in the fact that Ebadi, a former judge, was the first-ever Iranian and the first Muslim woman to have received the Peace Prize.

"In Iran, besides Muslim, any other traditions? Hindus or some Christians?" the Dalai Lama continued his focus on Ebadi.

"We do not have Hindus or Confucians, but we do have Jews, Christians, Zoroastrians, and Bahá'ís," Ebadi replied through her translator. "I wish I could invite you to travel to Iran, because there is something really interesting that I would like to show you. In Iran, there are many mystical sects."

"Sufis," the Dalai Lama said, with a hint of wonder in his expression. He leaned sideways at an acute angle, his torso propped up against an armrest of his chair. His right hand, curled in a loose fist, supported his listing head at the temple. He seemed unusually relaxed and mellow.

"I have visited one of these orders from a very close distance," Ebadi said, through her Iranian translator. "When they go through repeated invocation of God and repetition of whirling movements, they perform acts that are not logically explicable. I was present in one of their séances. When they whipped their passion into ecstasy, they began inserting swords into themselves so they would come in on one side and out another, without a drop of blood being spilled."

The Dalai Lama shook his head gently.

"One, however, was not able to elevate himself to a state of pure ecstasy," Ebadi continued through her translator. "When his guidance sheikh tried to help him insert his sword, I saw one drop of blood. Then they brought out knives with long handles and long blades, and they plunged these knives into their heads all the way to the handle."

The Dalai Lama stuck his tongue halfway out of his mouth when he heard this. His expression was of pure incredulity.

"How long?" he asked, spreading the fingers on one hand wide to make a guess at the length of the implement. Then he smacked his palms together resoundingly in front of his face. He had difficulty comprehending the astonishing act.

"And with the knives in the heads, they start the *sama*, the whirling dance, the Sufi dance," the translator concluded.

"Trance," the Dalai Lama stated.

"Yes, a state of trance," the translator affirmed.

"Among the Hindus, too," the Dalai Lama said. Turning to Reb Zalman, he asked, "Any among Jews?"

"Some," the rabbi replied. "Most of the time, we have given that one up. We are doing a lot more with prayers and meditation. But some talk about the soul leaving the body and going into other realms, doing what they need to do there."

"I recently met old nun from Tibet," the Dalai Lama said. "In her seventies and now living in Dharamsala. She told me she had some very mysterious experiences. She saw many strange things while she was in out-of-body experience. When young, she spent some time in mountain near Lhasa. There she met old monk, maybe eighty, teacher of few disciples. She said she saw two of them flying through the air down the mountain, spreading their robes like wings. She said she actually saw them flying for one kilometer. I was very surprised. But I think she had no reason to lie."

Herein lay a conundrum for the Dalai Lama. He had no doubt that the old nun was completely honest. I've come to know many Tibetans well over the years, and I'm convinced that they could no more lie to the Dalai Lama than harm their own families. But the Dalai Lama has a very analytic and critical mind. And he has been working closely with leading scientists in physics, psychology, and neuroscience over the last three decades. He is a great believer in empiricism and the scientific method. It was a big leap for me to believe that he would subscribe to the idea that a man could fly. Even if the man was an advanced mystic. The Dalai Lama once suggested to an interviewer that the only way a Buddhist monk could fly is by jumping off a cliff, spreading his robes, and hoping for a soft landing.

But then the Dalai Lama has himself witnessed certain phenomena that his rational mind finds hard to explain. Some years ago, he told me about the unusual circumstances that surrounded the death of his senior tutor, Ling Rinpoche, who died at the age of eighty-one on Christmas Day, 1983. Although Ling Rinpoche was clinically dead—his breathing had stopped and there was no pulse—he remained in some form of meditation for thirteen days. During this time, the area around his heart remained warm, and his body, unmoving in a meditative pose, showed no signs of deterioration. On the last day, his head dropped and a small amount of blood escaped from his nostrils. The Dalai Lama believed that it was only then that Ling Rinpoche's consciousness finally left his body. During the last few decades, the Dalai Lama has known of quite a few high lamas in Dharamsala and in other parts of India who showed similar behavior at death. He was sufficiently intrigued by these incidents that he asked a close friend, the eminent neuroscientist Richard Davidson from the University of Wisconsin, to assemble a team of researchers and doctors to look into the phenomenon.

NINETY PERCENT
PROJECTION

The Dalai Lama faced Aaron Beck across a glass-topped coffee table in a hotel room in Göteborg, Sweden. The Dalai Lama said, "You're older than me, so from the Buddhist or Asian tradition, the younger one must respect." Then he bowed slowly and deeply from the waist, like a Japanese Zen master.

Beck was taken by surprise and didn't know how to respond to the gesture. He stood there grinning awkwardly. The Dalai Lama bent down once more, this time to retrieve a ballpoint pen lying on the floor, and placed it on the coffee table between them. Beck picked it up and held it in his hands, together with his notebook.

Beck was eighty-six years old in June 2005 and had snow-white, close-cropped hair. Sixteen years older than the Dalai Lama, he was trim, fit, and immaculately dressed. He wore an expensive gray suit, pressed white shirt, and a striking red bow tie. I had learned the art of tying a bow tie at school in Hong

Kong and knew it had probably taken some nimble maneuvering on Beck's part to put it on that morning.

The Dalai Lama and Beck were in Göteborg at the invitation of the International Congress of Cognitive Psychotherapy. They were meeting at the Dalai Lama's hotel room to plan what they would say to each other, how they would sequence their public interaction later that afternoon before fourteen hundred attendees.

Beck began by presenting the Dalai Lama with a copy of a *Life* magazine from 1959, which had a cover photo of the Dalai Lama receiving flowers from his supporters after his escape from Tibet. Then Beck handed him a copy of his own newly published book, *Prisoners of Hate.*

The Dalai Lama took the book in his left hand and traced his right index finger across the title. He stared at the dust jacket, fascinated.

"Very good," the Dalai Lama finally said. "So from the viewpoint of this word, I think the entire six billion human beings are prisoners."

I was sitting behind him and saw that his index finger had lingered on the word "hate."

Beck replied, "We are all prisoners. Six billion prisoners."

The Dalai Lama leaned back and laughed heartily, somehow finding Beck's response hilarious. Beck settled into the couch and crossed his arms, pleased with the exchange and the Tibetan's reaction.

"Maybe hopefully some prisoners' sentences shorter," the Dalai Lama continued. "After, say, thirty years, or forty years, then becoming more wise, more compassionate. That means they no longer are prisoners."

Prisoners of Hate examines our tendency to engage in destructive behavior, and explores the relationship between our thinking processes and the resulting emotional expressions. Beck believes that people who descend into uncontrollable fits of rage and violence do so because of a distortion of their cognitive processes. Minor flaps get misinterpreted. As we begin to think of ourselves as victims, we respond by lashing out. A classic case of turning a molehill into a mountain.

The book is a distillation of the psychological insights Beck had gleaned over five decades. He is well known as the father of cognitive behavior therapy (CBT), a proven and powerful methodology to treat depression and other mental disorders. CBT emphasizes the importance of self-control and the regulation of impulses. It is today the most popular, and rapidly growing, form of psychotherapy. In 2007, Beck was short-listed for the Nobel Prize in Physiology or Medicine.

Beck scooted to the edge of the couch and took out his notebook. "Your Holiness, I thought I should start off . . ." he began. There was a touch of shyness in the demeanor of the world-famous psychiatrist that was surprising. He was not exactly the larger-than-life person I had expected. "I think you would like me to do the introduction on stage. I'd mention similarities between Buddhism and cognitive therapy. We would then go into problems we both see, like negative thinking."

"What is the definition when you use the word 'negative'?"

"We actually use the word 'errors,' errors in thinking. When we overgeneralize, say, He is bad because he did something I don't like, so he is a bad person."

"Right. Very true."

"Then how do we help people? Focus on the present, the moment. Okay?"

The Dalai Lama nodded. "And reflection," Beck continued, keeping his pale blue eyes steady on the Tibetan. "That means we are distancing ourselves from our emotions. We see anger as a cloud; we put it way out there. The word we use is 'distancing,' is this okay?"

"So that means when anger develops, you try to separate from the anger," the Dalai Lama said.

"Exactly. You're suffering from the anger. You separate yourself from the anger and then you examine the anger."

"Yes, that's right," the Dalai Lama said, leaning forward in his armchair and gesturing, his voice going up a couple of notches. "Usually when these negative emotions develop, then your whole self become like that emotion. So when this strong emotion develops, try to separate yourself from that emotion. Then can watch that emotion. Then much easier to see the faults of the emotion. Look from distance and that emotion's intensity weaken."

"Exactly. We also try to analyze where it comes from. It comes from the negative thinking." Beck was laying out the foundation of CBT for the Dalai Lama. "I think I have been wronged; you did wrong to me. So I have to examine: Did you really wrong me? You may not have, I may have misunderstood what you did, so we have to analyze. And then the second thing is: Even if you did wrong, does that make you a bad person? And, if you are a bad person, do I have to kill you, do I have to punish you? So that is the whole sequence."

⌘

A couple of years ago, I spoke to perhaps five hundred people in a full theater in Vancouver, about the intersection of science and spirituality. During the talk, out of the corner of my eye, I saw someone stand up and walk out. It so unnerved me that I started to have trouble remembering what I had to say; I didn't have any notes to fall back on, as I usually speak without them. I was jolted out of my comfort zone, trying desperately to remember the next point. My mind went blank and I started to stammer.

"Someone just walked out on me." "He thought I was an atrocious speaker." "He had trouble understanding my Chinese-accented English." All these thoughts reverberated in my head.

I turned my back to the audience and walked stiffly to the back of the stage, took a series of deep breaths, calmed down somewhat, and returned to the microphone. I was shaken, but I stumbled through the evening without another incident.

Later, when I got home, I realized that what had gone through my head onstage was not rational. I know I am a reasonably competent speaker, but paranoia had set in when the man got up and left. Things had become distorted in my mind. A more reasonable, and much less devastating, assumption would have been that he had to leave because he had another engagement.

Although I knew nothing about CBT at the time, I had inad-

vertently stumbled onto, and made good use of, its core princi-
ples that night. For Beck, the driving forces of our psychological
malaise are ideas that are unrealistic and self-defeating. He called
them "automatic thoughts." Like tinted lenses, they can color
and warp people's perceptions and affect their reactions.

Sitting directly behind the Dalai Lama in the Göteborg hotel
room, I could sense the intensity of the Dalai Lama's engagement with Beck. He was deeply focused on what the psychiatrist
had to say about the methodology of cognitive behavior therapy. And he was fascinated by how it helps patients confront
disturbing life situations realistically, with less debilitating distortion. He shifted in his chair, made himself more comfortable, and wrapped his maroon shawl around his shoulders more
securely.

"This therapy . . . similar to what Buddhists call analytic
meditation," the Dalai Lama said. It was giving him great comfort to know that the age-old insights of Buddhist mind-training
seem to have this parallel in Western psychology.

"What is it called?" Beck didn't catch the term.

"Analytic meditation. When emotion comes, use analytic
meditation to not let it dominate or influence. But rather analyze its consequences, its benefits, its destructiveness."

"I never knew about analytic meditation," Beck said. "So I
just learned that."

He consulted his notes and continued in his quiet voice, "Then we have selfishness. There is another word that we use, when we want to get away from our own selfishness, not to center everything on ourselves but try to center it on other people. The term we use is 'de-centering.' That sounds okay to you? Get away from the center?"

"Yes, actually one important Buddhist method is switching, exchanging oneself for others."

"So that is similar," Beck said. "Now, this self-centeredness we call 'egoism.' The big problem is the group—group violence, one group against the other group. We believe that the same self-ishness, the same self-centeredness, that we have in ourselves then gets expanded into the group. So now, instead of me being all good, you being all bad, my group is all good and your group is all bad. And my group has to exterminate your group so that everything will be good. So we are prisoners of our own hate. But they feel the same way about us—they feel they are all good and we are all bad. So we are all six billion prisoners. So this is cognitive therapy."

Beck leaned back into the couch and crossed his arms. He looked proud and contented; much of his shyness around the Tibetan had dissipated. It was clear that he was glad he was able to present the thesis of his new book to the Dalai Lama in a nutshell.

"Wonderful, wonderful," the Dalai Lama responded enthusiastically.

He was having a great time; there was a real and instant

chemistry between the two men, even though they had just met. I have not seen many of these energetic connections and meeting of minds in my years of travels with the Dalai Lama.

Nobody spoke for a while. Both men were basking in comfortable silence and well-being, a coming together of true kindred spirits.

"So one trivial question. Who created that prison?" the Dalai Lama eventually asked Beck.

"The original Buddhu. The Buddhu. He got out of the prison," Beck replied hesitatingly. Beck had misheard the question. He meant to answer that the Buddha got out of prison. But he got a bit flustered, and mispronounced the word "Buddha."

"No, no. Who created the prison?" the Dalai Lama repeated.

"Oh, who created the prison? I thought you meant who got out of the prison. I think that comes from evolution," Beck said.

The Dalai Lama was surprised but totally enamored with the answer. He threw his head back, laughed uproariously, and said, "That's right, that's right.

"So as a scientist, do you, some kind of . . ." The Dalai Lama wasn't able to find the words to frame his question. He asked the question in Tibetan, and Geshe Lhakdor, his translator, said, "His Holiness was wondering—in some fields of science do the scientists try to accommodate one's own scientific findings with the notion of believing in a creator god? In your case, do you try to harmonize such . . . ?"

"You mean God," Beck replied. "You once said that when the scientists prove that there is a god, then I will believe it. But they haven't disproven it, either."

"That's right, that's right," the Dalai Lama said.

"So take your choice."

"You are neutral." The Dalai Lama wanted to make sure.

"Neutral, yeah. But you don't need God to be a good person. In fact . . ."

"Ah, that is my approach," the Dalai Lama said with great satisfaction. "Usually my approach is secular ethics. Religious belief not necessary. Through analytic meditation, or through use of our common sense, you can be warmhearted person."

"Exactly."

"That is the way."

"Exactly, we take responsibility for ourselves, we don't need to look up to him," Beck said, and pointed at the ceiling.

"That's right."

"Look at how many people have been killed because of religion. Marxism is another religion. Whenever we are right and they are wrong, people get killed. So we have to be good people, not right people."

"Wonderful, wonderful." The Dalai Lama was enthralled.

"What we try to practice is: What is good for me, but should also be good for everybody," Beck added.

"That's right."

"If I only think of what's good for me, it may not be good for you."

"True, that's right, that's right."

"If I just think only of me, then I'd never think of you." Beck was on a roll. "Same thing with anger. If I'm angry with you, I'd tell you I'm angry at you. You can explain to me why you did not treat me well. You may have a good reason not to treat me well. And maybe I'm wrong. When people get angry, I'd say at least ninety percent of the time, the person who gets angry is wrong. That's my opinion."

"That's right," the Dalai Lama agreed. "Once I think negative emotion, afflictive emotion . . . once afflictive emotion develop, then you can't see the reality."

"Exactly."

"Strong mental projection. So here, Buddhist psychology quite clear explanation. The procedure, how these negative emotions are developed . . ."

"So for example . . ." Beck was unable to finish his thought. The Dalai Lama was so stimulated by what the psychiatrist had just said that he did not allow the interruption. "So, I entirely agree with your statement that ninety percent actually exaggerated. It's nearly all mental projection."

There was a heightened energy in the room; Beck was more than ready to jump in and make his point.

"And that is really true," Beck said. "When I get angry, I first think I'm wrong, not from a moral standpoint but from a reality standpoint."

A loud "That's right!" came from the Dalai Lama.

"My reality is wrong."

"That's right."

"You got it."

"Great teacher, great teacher," the Dalai Lama said.

I could tell that the Dalai Lama was impressed by this theory of ninety percent projection.

Beck was flushed from this animated exchange. He consulted his notes again.

"And then we should talk about addiction," he said. "When people are addicted—to food, or drugs, or to success, control— they can never be satisfied, because they are always overstimulated. And so, as soon as I satisfy myself, I cannot be contented because I'm overstimulated. I still think of success. As long as I think of success, or food, or drugs, I'm always going to want more and more. So I'm always going to be driven. And attachment to other people. If I'm too much in love, then I can't think. If I want too much success, fame, glory, then I can never get them, never feel satisfied. What does Buddhist philosophy say?"

"The same," the Dalai Lama said. "Being caught up in desire is like drinking salt water. The more you drink, the more you get thirsty."

"That's right, that's right. Going to write that down. That's good, it's like salty water, right."

The two elderly men, both extraordinary scientists of the mind, stood up and embraced. The Dalai Lama solemnly and carefully touched his forehead to Beck's as a gesture of supreme respect.

THE INCREDIBLE
STILLNESS OF A
PENALTY SHOOT-OUT

Murray Gell-Mann had celebrated his eightieth birthday two weeks earlier. Dressed in a gray suit and turquoise shirt, he sat hunched over the edge of his black leather armchair on the stage next to the Dalai Lama, his curly, snow-white hair clinging to his head like a closely fitted helmet.

"The great museum curator Kirk Varnedoe was also an enthusiastic rugby player," he told the Dalai Lama in a rich baritone, a trademark twinkle in his eye. "He compared modern art to the invention of the game of rugby. It happened one day early in the nineteenth century at Rugby School in Britain."

Sir Ken Robinson, seated to Gell-Mann's left, perked up. For twelve years, he had been a professor of arts education at the University of Warwick, England, a stone's throw from the town of Rugby. He seemed amused that Gell-Mann, a world-renowned physicist, would bring up the genesis of rugby football in this dialogue on creativity with the Dalai Lama. Eckhart Tolle, the spiritual teacher and author, sitting next to the Dalai Lama's translator, smiled.

Gell-Mann continued, "A soccer player decided to pick up the ball instead of kicking it . . . a fine disregard for the rules, thus founding the new game of rugby. Varnedoe pointed out that in modern art, you don't play by the rules, you play with the rules, and that's an aspect of creative thinking."

The Dalai Lama had some trouble understanding the story. Maybe he was confused by the unfamiliar-sounding names of Varnedoe and rugby; maybe he had never heard of the game before. His longtime translator, Thupten Jinpa, seated next to him, quietly explained.

Gell-Mann never ceased to amaze. Here he was, bringing up Varnedoe, a deceased art historian and not exactly a household name, in Vancouver in 2009, in a public event with the Dalai Lama. And in the same breath, he connected the arcane anecdote of the founding of rugby football to an element of creativity. I have met the famous physicist a number of times and I have always been in awe of his encyclopedic knowledge, not just of science but also of art, philosophy, politics, and religion. Gell-Mann has dominated the field of particle physics since the mid-1950s, when he was only in his twenties. He was awarded the Nobel Prize for Physics in 1969 for his work on elementary particles. One of his colleagues commented that Gell-Mann was not particularly known for his prowess in physics, but he was so universally brilliant that when he decided to apply himself to the discipline, he became a global sensation. In the early 1980s, he and several influential scientists founded the Santa Fe Institute, bringing together under one roof the most spectacular and eclectic intellectual firepower in America. He served as its first chairman and has been its éminence grise ever since.

The Dalai Lama had digested the connection between rugby and creativity and looked expectantly at Gell-Mann. The physicist was not done with his musings. He obviously took great delight in trying to make sense of creativity—another of the numerous subjects in which he has a keen interest—in the presence of the Dalai Lama.

"In theoretical science, which is the kind of thing I've done most of my life, most of the challengers to scientific orthodoxy are not right," he told the Dalai Lama. "Many of them are cranks. But every once in a while, scientific orthodoxy is wrong and one has to challenge it. It's not easy, going against convention. Your papers won't be published, you won't get a job. But sometimes you've got to do it. You've got to challenge orthodoxy."

Gell-Mann's thick, almost white eyebrows moved in concert with the deep furrows of his brow. His expressive and warm grandfatherly face belonged to someone at least a decade younger. His intellectual vitality was very much in evidence.

"But how do you get the idea of what to challenge?" Gell-Mann continued with his train of thought. "Well, it bubbles up from some hidden part of the human mind. There are several stages to it. Everybody agrees that if you have a problem, a contradiction, you ponder and try to resolve it. After a while, further conscious thought doesn't do any good. But somewhere out of sight, in some deeper part of the mind, this search for a solution continues. And one day, while cooking or shaving or running, or sometimes by a slip of the tongue, the answer may come to you."

The Dalai Lama leaned toward Gell-Mann, trying to understand what the physicist was saying. "It's that same deeper part of the human mind that's presumably involved in the search for how to educate the heart," Gell-Mann said. He seemed, uncharacteristically, less sure of himself at this point. He hesitated and stumbled over his words ever so slightly. He was venturing into uncertain territory. "This search for compassion is something that involves, at least occasionally, those parts of the human mind that are outside of conscious awareness. So there is possibly a relationship between creative thinking in art, in science, on one hand, and the search for compassion, forgiveness, on the other."

The Dalai Lama conferred briefly with his translator in Tibetan. He was sitting cross-legged in his armchair. His posture was informal. His back was hunched and he leaned forward in his chair so that his elbows and forearms rested on his thighs. It was as if, by orienting himself like this, he could absorb more of the conversation. But I could sense that his energy was flagging. He had just traveled from Los Angeles, where he had spent a few exhausting days.

"It seems to me that creativity is related more to intelligence," the Dalai Lama began tentatively. "Although I think other species of mammals also have it to some degree. A certain degree of creativity, but compared with human beings, much, much less. Why? Intelligence."

The Dalai Lama scratched the right side of his nose with his forefinger. He was deep in thought. I could see he was struggling to formulate a reasoned response.

The Dalai Lama continued, "Creativity is about creating new things, new things, new things. So it is mainly related to intelligence. Compassion is mainly related to . . . I don't know. Tibetan word is . . ." He told his translator the word he was looking for. "Compassion's qualities are related to the heart, but they tend to express themselves more in the form of a wish, an intent," Jinpa translated. The Dalai Lama listened carefully to the translation; he wanted to make sure that the nuances of what he wanted to say were conveyed accurately.

He continued in English, "Compassion is related to a wish, an intent. But its relationship with creativity is, I think, different. It is not direct. That means I feel . . ." Then another thought struck him and he changed his approach. "Then creativity. There also can be realistic creativity and unrealistic creativity. In most cases, unrealistic things are usually destructive, realistic things more positive. By positive I mean if you want something, even if you want to harm someone, the method to do so should be realistic. This way you will be more effective."

The Dalai Lama has always attached great importance to developing a realistic approach to life, to our interaction with others around us. He thinks that seeing reality accurately and unflinchingly contributes to our sense of well-being. It is a helpful antidote to distorted thinking.

"So, therefore, in order to develop a realistic approach, we have to know the reality fully," the Dalai Lama said. "In order to know the reality fully, an objective attitude is very essential. For that reason, calm mind is important. With calm mind, compassion develops. Compassion opens our mind, gives us wide perspective. With calm mind, you can see reality more clearly. With too much emotion, you can't see the reality. Creativity, mainly associated with intelligence. Compassion mainly with warm heart, so I think they are two separate things."

He paused for a moment and said, "But I really don't know."

The Dalai Lama stopped speaking and reached for his monk's bag on the low table in front of him. With great concentration, he started to search for something within it. This went on for some time as he had some difficulty finding what he wanted.

Eckhart Tolle, seated on the Dalai Lama's left, cleared his throat. He seemed to be rousing himself from a semi-meditative state. For much of the exchange, he had been sitting in his armchair with his eyes half closed and his hands clasped on his lap.

He opened his gray-blue eyes fully and said to the Dalai Lama, "We started off by talking about the genesis of rugby." His voice was soft, feminine even, and German-accented. "When I heard that, something came to mind, a news item that I heard a few days ago on BBC, my favorite news channel, and I believe Your Holiness's, too."

The Dalai Lama paused in his rummaging and smiled warmly at Tolle. It was quite a smile. One moment he was preoccupied with looking for something in his maroon bag, and the next he was flashing a smile of unadulterated friendliness at Tolle.

This was the first time the German and the Tibetan had met. I was quite sure that the Dalai Lama had no knowledge of Tolle's vast influence among millions of spiritual seekers from around the world. His two landmark books, *The Power of Now* and *A New Earth*, were both *New York Times* bestsellers and had been translated into nearly forty languages. His webinars with Oprah Winfrey have been seen by more than 35 million people worldwide.

"The BBC news item was about soccer . . . football, soccer," Tolle continued. "Researchers had looked at a phenomenon in soccer that is called, I believe, the penalty shoot-out. I haven't watched a soccer game in about twenty years, so I only have a vague recollection." Tolle's voice was mesmerizing. Quiet, very slow, and very friendly. The long pauses between sentences were hypnotic. Some listeners might find it too soothing, even sleep-inducing. "It is often the decisive moment in a game, and there's enormous pressure at this moment on this player, everything depends on it, sometimes an entire nation is watching."

Tolle paused for a long moment before saying, "So it's of incredible importance, not on a cosmic scale, but on a relative scale."

Jinpa leaned close to the Dalai Lama and explained the intricacies of the penalty shoot-out in a whisper.

Tolle continued, "The researchers examined what happens when the referee blows his whistle. Those players who do not pause, who immediately shoot after they hear the whistle, are much less likely to score than those players who, when the whistle goes, they don't immediately . . . there's three, four, five seconds, even more, when they become still. And when they finally shoot, the likelihood of scoring is infinitely greater than for those players who do not stop."

The Dalai Lama had finally found what he was looking for: his orange visor. He adjusted the Velcro clasp and put it on to shield his eyes from the harsh stage lights.

"The attention on the desired outcome, the attention on 'I have to perform,' this attention is taken away from all that," Tolle continued. "There is a redirecting of attention into the depths, into the moment. This I believe is the basis of the creative process: a redirecting of attention within. You touch a deeper level of your being, a deep, intensely alive stillness. And that is where all power resides. And when you touch that power, all conceptual things, including the concept of me, goes."

Tolle closed his eyes. He sat slumped forward in his chair, a picture of pure concentration. His pale green jacket was a couple of sizes too large for him. Although he is more than sixty years old, his face still retained an unmistakable trace of boyishness and innocence.

Tolle said to the Dalai Lama, "Now, this does not mean that when I'm asked to kick the ball and I go deeply within I'd score. Now, why not? I've gone deeply within, I've contacted the source of power . . . and it is not working." The Dalai Lama laughed quietly, his shoulders jiggling with mirth. "Something has to be prepared. Malcolm Gladwell referred to it in *Outliers*. To achieve proficiency, one prerequisite is ten thousand hours of practice. After ten thousand hours, we are ready to be receptive to the power of creativity."

Sir Ken Robinson, debonair in a dark suit and purple tie, looked sideways at Tolle with an expression akin to skepticism. He said to the Dalai Lama in his beautifully modulated Oxbridge accent, "I'm trying to shake off this image of Eckhart on a football pitch."

Without missing a beat, Murray Gell-Mann said, with mock contrition, "I really started something. I'm sorry. I take it all back."

"And the referee blows the whistle," Sir Ken continued, "and Eckhart waits ten thousand hours . . . and he still misses."

In one seemingly effortless aside, Sir Ken brought the house down. With his pitch-perfect timing and deadpan sense of humor, the celebrated educator could easily make a good living as a stand-up comedian. Over the last couple of years, I've watched his marvelous TED talk on creativity and education half a dozen times. I never get tired of watching it. It is a model of clarity, levity, and transformational insight. Even my then thirteen-year-old daughter had downloaded the talk onto her iPod, the only lecture that had so far found its way into her music and video collection.

"Perhaps creativity is something we have by birth," the Dalai Lama speculated after the laughter died down. "Possibly given by nature. Because of this brain, the potential for creativity is there. But then, I think, it is necessary to provoke it. Sometimes, when life is easy, problem-free, then maybe creativity remains asleep. When there are more difficulties, more contradictions, then our intelligence becomes much more active. But my knowledge about creativity is very limited."

He paused and repeated what he had said earlier, "I really don't know"—this time with added emphasis.

When I first had the idea of putting this panel together, I had doubts about the wisdom of trying to engage the Dalai Lama on a topic like creativity. I was aware that there is no word for it in Tibetan. The Dalai Lama is single-mindedly focused on spiritual attainment and cultivating positive internal experiences. He has little affinity with creative pursuits such as music, art, and dance.

But then I was carried away by the fact that I was able to bring world-famous, larger-than-life personalities like Sir Ken, Gell-Mann, and Tolle, all with highly idiosyncratic perspectives on creativity, to the dialogue. They stressed the importance of creativity and how crucial it is to make it part of the curriculum for children everywhere. Sir Ken Robinson has said, "My contention is that creativity now is as important in education as literacy, and we should treat it with the same status."

The Dalai Lama feels the same way about compassion, so I thought there would be natural parallels, but I should not have been surprised that he found the discussion on creativity difficult to follow and repeatedly pleaded lack of knowledge. It was an effort for him to stay engaged; his heart was simply not in it. He had a lot of time for the panelists but felt he had little to add to the conversation. And shoehorning creativity into compassion proved too much of a stretch.

THE MAGIC TRICK

On the count of three, words we have all learned: *Tashi delek* . . . and a bow!" Craig Kielburger bellowed into the microphone. The Dalai Lama walked slowly onto the stage in Vancouver. Pandemonium broke out. Sixteen thousand starstruck teenagers stood up and screamed the Tibetan greeting *"Tashi delek!"* The noise was ear-splitting. Thousands of cell phones and digital cameras were thrust high in the air; thousands of pinpoint flashes streaked toward the maroon-robed figure standing at one end of Vancouver's hockey arena.

The Dalai Lama went up to Kielburger. Facing the crowd, he bowed deeply, his palms together and touching his face.

Kielburger, founder of the Canadian organization Free the Children, said, "We wish to present two gifts to you. The first is a commitment to fund a school for Tibetan children in India. You have called the gift of education the greatest gift of all. We also have a small gift to you, something to symbolize our commitment to the world."

A fourteen-year-old girl approached the Dalai Lama and handed him a brown T-shirt. It was the same T-shirt— emblazoned with the famous words popularized by his hero Mahatma Gandhi, BE THE CHANGE—that Kielburger wore. The Dalai Lama touched it briefly to his forehead and slung it over his right shoulder. The crowd roared a second time. He was touched, and not a little surprised, by the enthusiastic reception. I couldn't recall another time when he was greeted with such explosive energy, usually reserved for the likes of Justin Bieber or Jason Mraz, who had warmed up the crowd for him.

The Dalai Lama gestured for the students to sit down. He turned and walked with Kielburger to the white sofas set up at center stage. He was wearing flip-flops.

"We have with us a group of children who have some questions for you," Kielburger said to the Dalai Lama as they held hands and sat down together.

"I love questions," the Dalai Lama replied. He released his grip on Kielburger's hand, shoved the fold of his robe up his arm, and looked at his watch. Kielburger smiled and there was a ripple of giggles from the crowd.

It was eleven-thirty a.m., and the Dalai Lama had just arrived at the arena after a hectic morning with an event at another venue. I had told Kielburger that he would have only ten minutes with the students. The Dalai Lama's schedule in Vancouver was brutal, and every minute was accounted for with military precision. He was already late for lunch, his last and most important meal of the day. I had no doubt that the Dalai Lama was famished (he ate breakfast six hours earlier) and his private secretary anxious to get him back to the hotel.

"May I ask for the first question," Kielburger said to the small group of students sitting cross-legged on the floor of the stage.

"Your Holiness . . ." a boy began.

The Dalai Lama hesitated; he conferred briefly with Thupten Jinpa, his translator, who was seated beside him.

"Oh, oh," the Dalai Lama interjected, "first let me say a few words."

"Of course," Kielburger said immediately. I knew he was surprised and a bit apprehensive by this turn of events. I had drilled him repeatedly on the procedure and time line. The private secretary had made sure of it. But Kielburger had no choice but to go with the flow at this abrupt change of script.

A thought struck the Dalai Lama. He said, "I want to talk from here, to stand." He stood up and went to the edge of the stage. The crowd went wild again. An avalanche of flashes lit up the arena once more. Kielburger slid off the sofa and sat down on the floor with the group of students.

"Dear young brothers and sisters," the Dalai Lama addressed the crowd. "I am extremely happy to spend few more minutes with you. This activity some kind of refreshment for me. I'm getting older, so mixing with young, bright, beautiful faces, I myself also feel, 'Oh . . . I maybe also one of them.'" He bent down and waggled a finger at the students sitting in the front rows. He rocked gently on the balls of his feet, looking very pleased with himself.

"You are the seed of better future," he said. "Time never stands still. No force can stop that. But we have the opportunity to use time more constructively. Or more destructively, or just waste. It's up to us."

There was complete silence. There were no more camera flashes.

The Dalai Lama continued, "Looking back twentieth century, human inventions in so many fields, particularly in technology, in science, really wonderful century. But it is also the century of most bloodshed. Some expert say over two hundred million human beings killed through violent action. All these people just like us, their lives precious to them, to their friends and family. Some use violence hoping to solve some problems, hoping to gain some good things. Now we look back: only suffering, only painful experiences. Therefore this century should be century of peace."

The crowd roared its approval. The applause, interspersed with shrieks and whistles, was deafening.

"What is peace? Peace does not mean no longer any problems, no longer any conflict. Some differences, some conflicts always there. Peace means when there is conflict, use our common sense and our compassion to consider rest of humanity, our human brothers and sisters. With this, restrain using violence. That is genuine peace. But unless we individuals possess inner peace, difficult. Isn't it? Genuine world peace must come through inner peace. You are the key people who will shape this century, make more peaceful, make compassionate century."

When the Dalai Lama first entered the hockey arena, I was very conscious of how tired he looked. He had just flown in from California and had, earlier in the morning, participated in a two-hour dialogue on creativity with some very high-energy and stimulating personalities, including Sir Ken Robinson and Eckhart Tolle. He'd had some trouble relating to their highly nuanced, Western-centric theories. But now he looked like a different person as he engaged with the young people, as vital and powerful as someone a couple of decades younger. He was transformed by the collective goodwill of his youthful audience.

The Dalai Lama said, "Two things." He slapped a forefinger onto his outstretched left little finger for emphasis. "First we should develop concept of entire six billion human beings being part of 'we.'"

I stole a glance at Kielburger. He was trying hard not to appear overly thrilled. It was a losing battle, as a lopsided grin spread across his face. After all, he had coined the name for this Woodstock-style meeting for the young and idealistic: We Day.

A huge part of We Day was the celebration of the ability of youth and their schools to change the world. On the program with the Dalai Lama were global icons including Jane Goodall, Mia Farrow, Canada's governor-general Michaëlle Jean, and Nobel Peace laureate Betty Williams. To help the crowd digest these lofty messages, much of the day was devoted to music. Headliners included Jason Mraz, Sarah McLachlan, K'naan, and the Canadian Tenors.

We Day was conceived by Kielburger, then twenty-seven years old, as more than just one day of celebration and inspiration. It was part of an innovative yearlong program created to educate young people about global issues and to showcase their power to work for the greater good. Kielburger had said, "It's not just an event, it is really a movement." It was free of charge and open to any school that wanted to be part of the experience. In exchange, each school group and each student who attended were asked to commit to local and global philanthropic projects throughout the year. Kielburger believes that the movement is linked to an underlying philosophy: creating a community committed to positive change. He had said, "The eighties and the nineties were known as the 'me' generation. . . . We need to swing the pendulum back very far in the other direction, so people focus more on 'we.' And that has to start with young people."

The Dalai Lama still had the brown T-shirt draped over his right shoulder. It added an unexpected splash of color to his standard-issue monk's robe and reminded me of Parisian waiters, who casually carry white napkins on their shoulders. The Dalai Lama was getting more and more animated as he was carried along by the energy of the students. His arms and hands were in constant motion, adding emphasis to his ideas and words. Instead of standing upright, he stooped with exaggeration, intent on peering closely at the front-row faces of his young audience.

"The century-old concept of 'we' and 'they' outdated," he said. "Also today's reality: everything interdependent, in economy, in environment, and also our happiness. If wherever we go people showing smile, we feel happy. In places where people showing negative face, then we don't feel happy. So let us make the whole world, world of smiles. Trust develops. We have to make compassion the basis of our inner peace and recognize that rest of humanity also have the right to overcome suffering. So we need infinite affection. That we can develop."

I marveled at the attention span of the students. They did not fidget; they seldom chatted to one another. There were the occasional camera flashes, but by and large they were hanging on to the words of the Dalai Lama. The connection of the sixteen thousand teenagers to the seventy-four-year-old monk was remarkable.

I stole a glance at my now fifteen-year-old daughter Lina, who was sitting demurely on the stage with Kielburger and the small group of students. This was not the first time she had been in the Tibetan's presence. Six years earlier, in one of my interviews with the Dalai Lama at his home in Dharamsala for *The Wisdom of Forgiveness*, I had taken Lina, her younger sister, Kira, and my wife, Susanne along. During this meeting, the Dalai Lama's interest in and affection for children had been apparent.

"Your great father," the Dalai Lama had told Lina and Kira at the time, as he perched on the edge of his armchair in his audience room in Dharamsala, "wasted his whole time during his first interview with me a few days ago. He plugged his microphone by mistake into his tape recorder's earphone jack." He found the memory of the incident so hilarious that he flopped back on his armchair and laughed uncontrollably.

"So I recorded nothing that day, and of course I had a hard time remembering what His Holiness told me," I told my daughters. That had the effect of boosting the Dalai Lama's laughter to another level of intensity. Lina, sitting with her mother and younger sister on the couch next to the Dalai Lama's armchair, smiled shyly and fiddled with the long straps of her shoulder bag. Ngari Rinpoche, the Dalai Lama's youngest brother, sat next to me. He had a big grin on his face.

I noticed that the Dalai Lama, sitting in the lotus position on his armchair, was watching Lina closely. My elder daughter was bored with the questions and answers and she was trying to tie knots with the thin leather straps of her small shoulder bag.

The Dalai Lama reached over and took the bag from her. He put it on his lap and straightened out the straps. Then he put his left arm through one of the loops and twisted the strap around. The Dalai Lama seemed to have some difficulty with what he was trying to do. He stared at the twin loops, nonplussed. He said something in Tibetan to his brother. Ngari Rinpoche, glad to have something to do, immediately got out a string of prayer beads and took it over to him.

The Dalai Lama took the long string and put his left hand through it so that the beads hung from the wrist. With his right hand, he twisted the dangling loop, brought it back up and around his wrist once again. Then, with one fluid motion, he casually tugged the prayer beads free from the side. Like magic. I laughed. The Dalai Lama was watching Lina as she slowly broke into a big grin; her sister giggled.

Still sitting in lotus, he leaned over to Lina and took her left arm. He hung the string of prayer beads on her wrist, twisted it once, and looped it around her hand a second time. "No, no, no," he said as he realized he had twisted the beads the wrong way and the trick wasn't going to work. He tried a couple of other permutations. None was the right one. "This isn't it, this isn't it." He was getting flustered. Ngari Rinpoche gave his brother some pointers in Tibetan. The Dalai Lama took the beads back from Lina and practiced the trick on his own wrist. It came off as easily and elegantly as before. "Yes, yes," he said with satisfaction. Then he reached over and draped it around Lina's left arm once more.

This time, he pulled off the sleight of hand like a pro.

At the hockey arena in Vancouver, the Dalai Lama wanted to continue with his train of thought about infinite affection and compassion. "My own case: My mother very kind mother. My father not like that," the Dalai Lama confided, to the delight of the students. "I believe some amount of my compassion actually came from my mother. Not from teaching. Not from religion. The seed of compassion comes from mother."

"In Tibet, young child usually carried on mother's shoulder," he said. "I loved that and I held my mother's two ears, like that." He grabbed his ears with both hands to demonstrate. Then he lowered his hands, balled them into fists as if they were holding the reins of a horse. "Then when I want to go this side, do that." His right hand pulled the imaginary rein to the right. "Go that side, do like that." His left hand jerked forcefully to the left. "My mother so kind, that kindness spoil her young boy. So sometimes I become more aggressive. If mother don't listen my wish, I cry and do like that." The Dalai Lama tugged his hands rapidly and alternately.

The crowd went wild again. Thousands of camera flashes lit up the arena. One young girl in a yellow T-shirt looked at the spectacle of the Dalai Lama mimicking a spoiled toddler with undisguised wonderment. It was not exactly what she had expected from a world-famous religious teacher.

The Dalai Lama straightened up. In a heartbeat, the frivolity disappeared, and he was all business again. "We really receive genuine seed of compassion from our mothers. That's same for everybody. Take this seed and use our common experience, common sense. Latest scientific finding shows more compassionate person has better health. Not only peace of mind. Also very good for our physical health. Now finish. Some questions."

The Dalai Lama turned, walked back to his sofa, and sat down in the lotus position. Kielburger took a seat next to him.

An Asian girl, part of a small group of students sitting on the floor next to the Dalai Lama, raised her hand. Kielburger pointed at her and nodded.

"Your Holiness, *tashi delek*," the girl greeted the Dalai Lama in Tibetan. "How do you think we all learn to be more compassionate?"

The Dalai Lama was unsure of the question and turned to Jinpa for clarification. Kielburger tried to be helpful and said, "The question was: How do we all learn, how do you think we young people can all learn to be more compassionate?"

The Dalai Lama said, "That I already mentioned." A ripple of laughter from the crowd. Kielburger bowed and put his head in his hands in mock shame. He told the Dalai Lama, "They love your teaching and they all want more."

"We all have the seed of compassion," the Dalai Lama said with a slight touch of exasperation. He was being more tolerant and patient than I have seen him be in private. Since we know each other so well, if I had asked the same question, he would have told me bluntly that I had repeated myself, that I had not paid careful attention to what he had said earlier.

"We receive this seed from our mother. From our mother's milk. And this small thing, this little bump that we put into our mouth, what you call this?" He pointed a finger at his chest, stumbling as he tried to come up with the right word. Jinpa looked mortified, but plowed on dutifully: "Nipple."

"Nipple, yes. Like that." The Dalai Lama, with no self-consciousness whatsoever, stuck his forefinger in his mouth and proceeded to suck on it with great relish. His headset mike amplified and projected the loud, uninhibited sucking sound to the upper rafters of the arena. "So we already got full blessing of compassion from our mother. That is seed. Those young children who unfortunately lack affection from their parents or in some cases got abused, such children difficult to develop compassion. Real seed comes from mother. When you grow up, when you marry, when you produce young children, then please provide maximum affection to your children, that very important."

∾

I marveled at the Dalai Lama's insight about mother's milk. He fervently believes that the bond of affection is developed early between mother and child through the process of nursing. He suggested that this bond is the biological basis of genuine compassion. But the onus is on us to nurture it to full flowering, with intelligence and wisdom, as we grow older.

EDUCATING THE HEART

In a rare departure from his usual choice of topics, the Dalai Lama reminisced about the seasons. "In springtime, everything grows, there is new life, so we feel happy," the Tibetan spiritual teacher told a panel of education researchers in Vancouver in 2009. "In autumn, leaves fall down, trees become naked, so we consider autumn to be lesser than springtime, so that's indication of our basic nature. We want freshness, survival, growth, and peace."

He placed his hand lightly on his chest and said with feeling, "But peace lives not with intelligence, but here, with warmheartedness."

"Now, everybody knows there is something lacking in education," the Dalai Lama said to Kimberley Schonert-Reichl, an education professor at the University of British Columbia. "Education is a key factor to a happier, peaceful human society. So we need specialists like you. Need more research, and then concrete ideas and proposals. Several times in Europe and in America, also in India, I have expressed these things. At the time people agree, fully agree. But then nothing happened. Now time running out, so some proposal should come. Do not expect it to come from me. No. I do not know anything. No. It is up to you educated people, you are professor."

"Well, you know, we basically have been doing a lot of research," replied Schonert-Reichl, a bubbly woman with a dazzling smile. "When you were in Vancouver three years ago, you told us to 'just get to work now.' A lot has happened since. There are now many initiatives that focus on educating the hearts of children."

"I want to know," the Dalai Lama said, "this practice of education of the heart, in the results level, what differences have you found? Between those students who haven't had that kind of education, and those who have passed through that kind of education? What are the differences?"

The question was unusually direct for the Dalai Lama. It might well have come from a hard-nosed research scientist asking for empirical evidence from a colleague. Even as a young boy, the Dalai Lama was blessed with a questioning, analytic mind. Nearly three decades ago, he cofounded the Mind & Life Institute, which is dedicated to organizing dialogues between the Dalai Lama and scientists and scholars to promote a deeper understanding of the nature of the mind, emotions, and reality. All these years of interaction with acclaimed physicists, psychologists, and brain scientists have given him a distinctive man-of-science aura.

"We have developed programs for both students and teachers

that promote mindful attention awareness," Schonert-Reichl reported. "We are finding differences in children who receive these programs. They develop empathy, altruism, compassion. They even do better in school. So we know there are a lot of good things that happen when we educate heart and mind together."

"Wonderful!" the Dalai Lama said. I could see that he was glad that his multiple visits to Vancouver had yielded tangible outcomes. Schonert-Reichl was grinning broadly. She had developed a twelve-month program to teach pre-service teachers about educating the heart, the first in North America. These teachers-in-training learned how to incorporate social and emotional development into every type of subject. Evidence has shown that they welcome this holistic approach to education and identify it as an area where they have a critical need for more guidance.

In 2010, U.S. researchers analyzed 213 studies involving nearly 300,000 students in elementary and middle schools. They found that those students who received social, emotional, and mindfulness instruction scored 11 to 17 percentage points higher on achievement tests, compared with those who did not receive such instruction. The students also felt better about school and behaved more positively. The result? Fewer incidents of alcohol and drug use, violence, and bullying.

For the past several years, Schonert-Reichl has also worked closely with actress Goldie Hawn to study the effectiveness of the Hawn Foundation's pioneering MindUP program. This is a fifteen-module curriculum designed by educators and brain scientists to promote mindfulness in the classroom. The data show that children who have completed the course improved their ability to concentrate. They experienced less stress and performed better on standardized tests. The students managed their emotions and behavior more effectively and developed greater empathy for others. Above all, they tended to be happier and more optimistic.

❧

I have been exposed to the idea of mindfulness since my childhood. When I was growing up in Hong Kong, my mother enrolled me in Chinese calligraphy and tai chi classes. At their core, both disciplines emphasize deliberation, precision, and one-pointed focus. Haste and sloppiness were frowned upon. I did not take to the painstaking and repetitive act of writing out complex Chinese characters using bamboo brushes dipped in lustrous lamp-black ink. In the kung fu studio, I was far more interested in the explosive movements of White Crane than the sleep-inducing stupor of tai chi. After a while, my mother gave up; I never did pick up those bamboo brushes again. But, after a long hiatus, I eventually continued with tai chi. The subtle rewards of mindfulness practice, the process of fostering an awareness of every sensation as it unfolds in the moment, had left an imprint on me.

Many years later, as I crisscrossed the Himalayas on foot researching my book on the sacred geography of Tibet, I walked for hours every day in mindful and blissful silence. As I made my way toward the top of a 19,000-foot pass, loaded with a fifty-pound backpack, I imagined myself walking on the waterlogged edge of a beach. I would bring my full attention onto each step and visualize leaving as shallow an imprint of my feet on the wet sand as possible. This simple technique centered me and held my "monkey" mind at bay. The snatches of euphoria that came from being "in the zone" lessened the physical and psychological discomfort of trekking long distances in high altitudes.

I have come to realize that I can enjoy the simple pleasures of mindfulness, those precious moments of well-being, without contorting my legs into a lotus position to meditate formally. Periods of mindful clarity can occur throughout the day. With discipline and perseverance, it is possible to cultivate a culture of one-pointed focus in most of our activities: chewing food twenty times before swallowing; slowly brushing our teeth, paying attention to each individual tooth; walking with deliberation, mindful of the rise and fall of each step.

I know it is possible to do all this and more in our daily life, to create a mindful culture, to bring about an antidote to the haste and the soul-numbing multitasking that are part of our zeitgeist. It is a good thing for our sons and daughters to incorporate versions of this into their school and family environment. Learning to be mindful is an essential element of "educating the heart"— it is a central tenet of the Dalai Lama's worldview and one of the most tangible, accessible ways of enhancing our well-being.

❧

For the Dalai Lama, educating the heart is an effective corrective to a world that embraces academic achievement with near-religious fervor. He believes that it is necessary to take a step back and look at the bigger picture, to examine a young person's interaction with his or her family, community, and the environment. Empathy and the ability to manage stress are skills that can help students lead a more fulfilled life. He believes that the classroom can be a place to nurture young people in becoming caring, tolerant, and peaceful individuals, not just a place to learn to read and write, add and subtract.

Although the Dalai Lama believes in the importance of cultivating mindfulness and enhancing social and emotional competencies—work that researchers like Schonert-Reichl and others are focused on—his perspective on education is far more nuanced. His ideal, and it is no doubt a lofty one, is to make sure that our youth understand the interconnectedness of all things, and as they mature, begin to experience all of humanity as brothers and sisters. For the Dalai Lama, educating the heart implies learning that leads to developing genuine compassion.

"There are two levels of compassion," the Dalai Lama told Schonert-Reichl. "One level has more to do with biological factors. This compassion needs no training. No need to get help from wisdom. It is spontaneous. Like compassion from mother to their children, or compassion between relatives—at least those relatives that show you a positive attitude. These are biological factors, and very much dependent on others' attitudes."

For the Dalai Lama, compassion or a feeling of closeness at this level could quickly turn into resentment and hatred. This is because it is tinged with attachment and desire. Romantic love, for instance, is often associated with self-centered emotional needs. When the going is good, we tend to exaggerate and over-emphasize our partner's good qualities. But when feelings or circumstances change, disappointment and a sense of betrayal are often the result. This kind of love is motivated more by personal need than genuine concern for the other.

The Dalai Lama cautions that our negative emotions are often impulsive, not based on an accurate reading of the situation. Our overly emotional responses hinder our ability to behave rationally and constructively. Positive emotions, however, are grounded in a realistic way of seeing and are conditioned by wisdom. True compassion, therefore, is not colored by emotions. It is a firm commitment that remains rock-solid even when we are confronted with hostile behavior.

The Dalai Lama now gave an example of his own prejudices when he was a small child. Whenever he came across two dogs fighting, his heart invariably went out to the one getting clobbered. He had to work hard to suppress his instinct to kick out at the stronger one. When he got older, he realized that his behavior showed a clear bias, a clear discrimination, in his practice of compassion.

"Now, second level of compassion is beyond that, it is based on understanding and respect," the Dalai Lama continued. "It's not dependent on the others' attitude. We disregard, pay less attention to how others treat us. We are mindful they are human beings, and they, like us, have feelings. I want happiness. I do not want suffering. Because of that, I have the right to work on eliminating suffering. But the other seven billion human beings have the same right. In today's interconnected reality, my future depends on others. So I have to take their interest ultimately as my own interest.

"When others are passing through difficulties, we must respond because we have a sense of concern for them. So this is genuine compassion, second-level compassion. It is stable and unbiased. It is oriented to the person, to someone who, like us, feels pain acutely."

As the Dalai Lama has said, it does not matter whether people are beautiful and friendly or unattractive and hard to get along with. The bottom line is that they are human beings, just like us. And like us, they crave happiness and do not want to suffer. Moreover, their right to overcome suffering and be happy is not less than ours. If we can internalize this universal truth, we should automatically feel empathy for them. It is through habituating our minds to this all-encompassing altruism that we develop a sense of responsibility for others. We ingrain within us the wish to help others overcome their difficulties. For the Dalai Lama, this aspiration is uniformly applied to all, without discrimination.

"Genuine compassion means we treat everyone same," continued the Dalai Lama. "We develop understanding and warmheartedness even to our enemies. This is true compassion. With this way we act with altruism. We care only for the welfare of others. Selfish motives do not influence the way we think or behave. As a Buddhist monk, cultivation of compassion is a daily practice. Usually I sit quietly in my room and meditate on lovingkindness."

For beginners, this simply means conjuring up the faces of

those we care deeply about—our children, for example. Usually, without much effort, we summon up a feeling of lovingkindness toward them. After some time, we replace these loved ones with friends and acquaintances. Then, eventually, with strangers. As the practice deepens, this feeling of affection is extended to include people who upset us.

The practice of this kind of meditation has been shown by Antoine Lutz and Richard Davidson, neuroscientists at the University of Wisconsin–Madison, to increase the ability to be compassionate. In their study of experienced meditators who were focused on compassion, fMRI scans showed that their brain region responsible for empathy, the left prefrontal cortex, became highly activated when they heard the sounds of a woman screaming or a baby crying. The meditators correctly identified and then empathized powerfully with the anguish that the woman and the baby experienced. A heightened sense of compassion was the result.

Prolonged practice of meditation apparently helps trigger a resonance with the emotional state of another person. Experienced meditators are able to replicate that emotional state, going beyond mere intellectual understanding, to produce a powerful wave of empathy and compassion. For them, the boundaries between "self" and "other" are blurred. As they go about their daily lives, there is an increased identification with those outside their immediate circle of close friends and family. They know that we are all one, and are relentless in working for the welfare of the "other."

Scientists were surprised to see that when these meditators

were in a stable state of contemplation, their neural circuitry associated with compassion was not the only area of their brains affected. The areas directly correlated to action—the motor cortex and the basal ganglia—also lit up with dazzling intensity.

❧

"Compassion is developed through training, through reasoning." The Dalai Lama continued speaking about his favorite topic. "Education has a very important role in cultivating it. But development of brain alone not certain to bring inner peace or happiness.

"One Tibetan monk I know well, he was a member of my monastery, and very close to me. Since 1959, he spent eighteen years in Chinese gulag. In early eighties, because of new situation, some Tibetans can come to India. This monk came and we met and we talked casually. Few occasions I met him. Then one day he mentioned during eighteen years in gulag he experienced some danger. I asked him what danger? He replied: Danger of losing compassion toward Chinese. This person not much education, not good scholar, but very good practitioner. He considered compassion toward so-called enemy very important, so he practiced that. He kept compassionate attitude toward the persons who create problems for him. Result: His mind very calm, very peaceful. Compassion gave him happiness."

A GENTLEMAN FROM
BANGLADESH

In 1970 there was a big cyclone in Bangladesh," Sir Fazle Hasan Abed told the Dalai Lama in Vancouver in 2009. The Bangladeshi was settled into an ample leather armchair, his legs comfortably crossed. "Three hundred thousand people died. I went out to the villages, dead bodies strewn everywhere. Suddenly it occurred to me that the life I was leading, working for Shell Oil, had no meaning. So I started working for relief and rehabilitation, focusing on the poorest of the poor." Abed spoke quietly and without embellishment. But he emphasized his points with fluid hand gestures, a slight smile playing on his face from time to time.

"I realized early on that helping the poor has to be a long-term commitment," Abed continued. "Development has to be multifaceted, holistic. It's more than just employment. It's not just education. It's a combination of all these things. I learned that people don't need to be objects of development, they need to be subjects of development. I believe that people can change their own lives themselves. So I created the Bangladesh Rural Advancement Committee, or BRAC. We took that philosophy and tried to organize people so that they are directly involved."

It had been, as usual, an intensely hectic day for the Dalai Lama. He was tired, his energy flagging, but, with his head craned in the direction of Abed, he was listening intently to what the Bangladeshi had to say about empowering the poor, a subject in which the Dalai Lama has a keen interest. I had put together this invitation-only meeting with the hope that accomplished humanitarians like Abed could tell their stories and explain their work to the Dalai Lama. Quite a few were relatively unknown, people who quietly and with great effectiveness transformed the lives of the poor. Among them were Frank Giustra of Vancouver; Ela Bhatt of India; and Susan Davis of New York, who had worked closely with Abed for many years. There were notable names as well: Bob Geldof, Peter Buffett, Pierre Omidyar, and Maria Shriver. They all had something in common—a desire to make a difference as expeditiously and as effectively as possible.

For the past couple of decades, the Dalai Lama has often said that his overriding priority in life is to foster values such as compassion, forgiveness, and altruism. He has traveled the world with this message, often at public lectures and panel discussions, but sometimes at mega-events with audiences of thousands.

But I had a sense that after stating his lifelong commitments over and over, he was feeling frustrated. He was disappointed that self-interest was still the norm and the gap between the rich and poor ever widening. I thought it worthwhile for him to be exposed to people who share his ideals but who also possess the skill sets and competence necessary to improve the lives of those whose survival is always tenuous.

Abed is a distinguished-looking man in his early seventies. With his carefully parted snow-white hair and somber pinstriped suit, he would not have been out of place in a multinational boardroom. I have known him for a few years and spent time with him in New York City, Vancouver, and Delhi. He was always the impeccable gentleman, unfailingly courteous and exuding low-key goodwill. But beneath his grandfatherly charm, I sensed a man of steel conditioned by a transcendental vision.

Abed realized that to bring about real change in Bangladesh, his scope had to be nationwide. Just working in one district would not be enough. When he founded BRAC, the country's population was approaching 100 million. He knew that he needed to grow his nascent organization fast. His experience at Shell Oil, the third-largest energy company in the world, was invaluable.

"I saw how they worked," Abed said. "Shell had worldwide operations and they were effective. So I thought, becoming large doesn't mean you have to be ugly. During the first ten years of BRAC, we were learning to be effective and how to expand quickly.

"For the last thirty-seven years, I have focused on poverty alleviation. We pioneered microfinance—we now have more than eight million women borrowers. We have given out five billion dollars in loans. We created schools—thirty-seven thousand so far—where all the teachers are women, and seventy percent of our two million students are girls. Above all, we focus on girls and women as agents of change in all our communities in Bangladesh."

Nicholas Kristof of *The New York Times* described BRAC as "an incipient movement to emancipate women and fight global poverty by unlocking women's power as economic catalysts. That is the process under way—not a drama of victimization, but of empowerment, the kind that transforms bubbly teenage girls from brothel slaves into successful businesswomen. This is a story of transformation." Abed and a more famous compatriot, Nobel Peace Prize winner Muhammad Yunus, have long understood the transformative power of women and girls when they are given the opportunity to go to school and enter the formal labor force. Abed exemplified that mission perfectly. I considered it a real coup to be able to bring him to Vancouver to meet the Dalai Lama.

❧

Abed, who began his career as an economist, had looked at all the available data and discovered that a girl who goes to school for at least seven years marries later and has fewer children. He learned that if the girl gets an extra year of primary school, it increases her eventual wages by 10 to 20 percent; an extra year of secondary school brings this up to 15 to 25 percent. He came to the conclusion that girls as agents of economic change can bring about long-lasting transformation for themselves, their families, and their communities. He had no doubt that the most effective strategy to combat global poverty, to ameliorate civil strife, even to improve the environment, was simply to invest in girls' education. Ignoring the potential of girls could cost societies billions.

But Abed was up against tremendous challenges. Bangladesh is a highly patriarchal society, and gender discrimination is rampant. Women have a much tougher time when it comes to access to education, health care, and accumulating wealth. Their traditional role is to produce babies and they are discouraged from participating meaningfully in all aspects of public life. The country has the highest rate of early marriage in Asia. A 2004 United Nations report estimated that nearly half of all girls between fifteen and nineteen years of age were married, divorced, or widowed.

Against this backdrop, what made Abed so passionate a champion of girls and women? "One face that comes to mind when I think of compassion is my mother," he explained to the Dalai Lama. "Her mind-set is different from that of most women in Bangladesh. When somebody is ill, you send medicine. My mother would not only send medicine. She would also send kerosene, so that the sick person would have the comfort of light. She would think through all the details, the myriad indignities that people suffer, and she would try her best to help. She was my greatest influence. It was because of her that I worked so tirelessly all these years in poverty alleviation and particularly in empowering women as agents of change."

"My mother also very kind," the Dalai Lama replied. "Basically uneducated, a farmer. Not only was she kind to her own children, she also kind to other people who lived in very difficult conditions. One time in China some famine happened. Thousands of poor people came through our village, many beggars. My mother gave them all the things in our home, mainly food, bread, these things. So wonderful. And I almost never saw her angry face. She was always calm."

The scope of BRAC's enterprise is mind-boggling. In 2010, it was recognized as the world's largest nongovernmental development organization. Since its inception in 1972, it has founded a microfinance commercial bank, an Internet service provider, a university. Its ninety clinics and more than two thousand prenatal centers provide health care throughout the country. It started a dairy to help farmers who could not get a fair price for their cows—it is now the country's second largest. It opened a chicken hatchery to supply the poor with 2 million chicks a month.

BRAC does all this and more without relying overly on foreign donors, as so many of the world's NGOs and others in the nonprofit sector tend to do. About 80 percent of its annual operating budget of half a billion dollars is generated internally. Over time, Abed has managed to cultivate a can-do culture in the organization. Efficiency is one of his mantras, and BRAC is run like a business, with targets to be achieved, whether it is reduction of mortality rates or increasing the numbers of children attending school.

Abed also likes to draw attention to what he calls the Bangladeshi character, a key component in the BRAC culture. "We have been very resilient, despite the problems we've faced. We have always risen and have never been defeated. We will fight until we get to where we want to be."

I could see that the Dalai Lama was impressed by the effectiveness and scale of Abed's work in the developing world. His own life is weighed down by multiple responsibilities, among them the welfare of the Tibetan people, his hectic travel schedule, and his frequent teachings. On top of all this he has to carve out precious time to focus on his spiritual practice. He is best known in the West for his work promoting compassion and nurturing what he calls a "kind heart." His vast Western audience invariably wants to hear about things that most concern them: how to cope with stress, how to live a meaningful life, and, above all, how to be happy.

But I know that his heart instinctively goes out to those who try to survive at the bottom of the pyramid. And I wonder whether, in the dark of the night, he ever dreams of shrugging off the burdens of his office to go barefoot into the slums and bring succor directly to the destitute. Did he ever consider taking a page from the playbook of Mother Teresa?

It is not often that the Dalai Lama comes across someone like Abed, someone whose mission is simply to improve lives. "I am a Buddhist monk and study Buddhist philosophy and also practice to some extent, hopefully," the Dalai Lama confided to Abed. "So my main field where I know something, where I have some sort of confidence, is emotion. Also motivation. That may be my professional field. Then, beyond that, my knowledge and experience is zero.

"So you who are really committed in action, I admire. I appreciate. Especially your foundation, when you explain your work, it really gives me some kind of confidence. If you help people work together, their lives can change."

After working and refining a holistic approach in Bangladesh, Abed and BRAC started a process of replicating the model in other countries. "Now, for the past seven years we have started going to other countries," Abed told the Dalai Lama. "We are in Afghanistan, Pakistan, Sri Lanka. We are in five countries in Africa. Most recently we went to Haiti. I find that poor people's dreams are more or less the same everywhere. What we do in Bangladesh works just as effectively in Africa." BRAC's programs currently have a direct impact on 138 million of the poorest people in ten countries. *The Economist* calls BRAC "by most measures the largest, fastest-growing non-governmental organisation in the world—and one of the most businesslike." And, surprisingly, perhaps the least known.

The Dalai Lama found compelling not just the idea of making a substantial difference in Bangladesh but the notion of exporting its best practices to other countries as well. "Not only help your own country but you also carry that experience to other difficult areas," he said to Abed. "I think that is the way forward. I really appreciate. And also, I think, it is easy to have great visions. But real step-by-step implementation, involving many complicated factors, not easy. So I admire your work.

"One thing, I think. Work closer together with other organizations, promote more cooperation using modern techniques. Your organization has experience and has learned ideas that are effective. Then teach other organizations. But there should not be repetition. And I think two, three organizations should constantly exchange views and experiences. Then they find new ideas, new methods. Then work together."

The following day, in an interview with the press, a journalist asked the Dalai Lama what he had learned in Vancouver. He replied, "One thing I wanted to share with you. I always admire the nongovernmental organizations. I think they very sincere, very dedicated. On the practical level, this kind of attitude, this kind of thinking, very good.

"Yesterday, in our meeting, I was very much impressed by one Bangladeshi gentleman. He started on a small level, an NGO. Then he gradually grew to a national level. Then, not only that, he exported his sort of expertise, his experience to other countries. That's wonderful, really wonderful. So what one single person initiates eventually can affect millions of people. So that's wonderful. That I learned."

A TEACHER IN SOWETO

The Dalai Lama has often told his mostly educated, white, middle-class Western audience that we need to develop our intelligence. But he insists that this must be complemented holistically with educating the heart, incorporating mindfulness and emotional and social competencies into our learning. He believes that these skills can give us self-confidence, success in life, and true happiness.

Sir Fazle Hasan Abed, the founder of BRAC, the world's largest nongovernmental development organization, and Susan Davis, the founder and president of BRAC USA, heard this message at the Vancouver Peace Summit of 2009, where they participated in discussions with the Dalai Lama.

It was the session with educators that was the most powerful for the BRAC founders. During that meeting, they were exposed to the latest research on the benefits of fostering emotional and social well-being in young people and, in particular, to the research of Kimberley Schonert-Reichl, at the University of British

Columbia. When they left Vancouver for Dhaka, this was the "Aha!" moment that stayed with them.

Educating the heart was an idea that the Dalai Lama had planted in Schonert-Reichl when they had first met in 2006. Now the ripple effect of his words was about to make itself felt halfway around the world in Bangladesh.

I have known Susan Davis for several years. We attended some of the same development conferences at Oxford, New York City, San Francisco, and Washington, D.C. She struck me as an unusually entrepreneurial woman, who exudes megawatts of goodwill. Since graduating from Harvard and Oxford, she has dedicated her life to helping the poor in developing countries.

"Fostering peace is a very important part of my work with BRAC," Davis told me. "Many of the places where we work are at war or were formerly at war. I came to understand that to create a culture of peace, it is vital that the most vulnerable children know how to deal with frustrations, humiliation, and anger. BRAC has been investing in the basic skills of reading, writing, and arithmetic. But from now on, thanks to the Dalai Lama, we will also look at social and emotional core competencies, like emotions regulation and relationship skills. We need to look at educating the heart along with educating the mind and the hands. I think this is the most important thing we can do at BRAC."

After the Vancouver Peace Summit, Abed and Davis hired a prominent U.S. education consultant to find out how the young children in BRAC's 37,000 schools in Bangladesh rate in social and emotional competencies. They wanted to know if the children were able to recognize their own emotions such as sadness, anger, and happiness. And whether they were able to tune in to the verbal and situational cues that signal how others feel in a social setting. Abed and Davis also wanted to know whether the children were comfortable approaching adults for help when they got into trouble. The consultant concluded that most of the kids had the self-confidence to do so, but about a quarter still had a long way to go.

After this initial assessment, Abed and Davis convened a system-wide workshop for the key personnel responsible for training BRAC's teachers. As a result of the meeting, BRAC's teaching curriculum was modified to include aspects of social and emotional learning (SEL).

But Abed didn't want to stop there. If SEL had proven to be so effective and important, he wondered, why limit it to education? He wanted SEL to be embedded within the vast system of BRAC so that its insights and protocols could benefit all of its 125,000 employees—a hugely ambitious undertaking. "Abed and I have been profoundly inspired by the Dalai Lama," Davis said. "We were moved by his call to find better ways to translate compassion into action. We try to do that at BRAC, and we measure it in the number of lives affected. The data show that we are touching the lives of 138 million people: their collective net worth has increased by fifty percent, their savings doubled, and their use of sanitary latrines went from nine to twenty-seven percent. Their lives are definitely better.

"But having heard from His Holiness in Vancouver, we are concerned about the quality of that touch. We need to look at more nuanced indicators of real empowerment, that sense of agency of personal power and inner well-being. We believe that educating the heart is critical."

I was surprised and heartened that a huge global organization like BRAC has committed to embracing a "fringe" idea like educating the heart, an idea that is just taking root in the West. Key thinkers, such as Daniel Goleman and Jon Kabat-Zinn, have been talking about this for a number of years. And now the movement is gathering momentum as major philanthropists, including Peter Buffett, Pierre and Pam Omidyar of eBay, and U.S. congressman Tim Ryan of Ohio, begin to embrace it with enthusiasm. Their collective vision would bring a focus of mindfulness, and SEL, into every classroom in North America. But BRAC? Bangladesh?

For people familiar with the world of development, this might not come as a surprise. Bangladesh has, over the decades, gained a reputation as the Silicon Valley of social innovation. It is home to two towering global figures, Fazle Abed and Muhammad Yunus—the Nobel Peace laureate and founder of the Grameen Bank, a pioneer of microfinance. And it has given birth to some of the most audacious and effective approaches to alleviating poverty that the world has seen.

In spite of its stunning scale and impact, however, BRAC remains one of the best-kept secrets in the development world. Davis told me ruefully, "When Barbara Walters learned about BRAC, she said, 'It can't be true. If I have never heard of BRAC, it can't be true.'"

But I have no doubt that BRAC's embrace of educating the

heart could have far-reaching implications. I can well imagine the profound effect that 125,000 dedicated workers fluent in social and emotional learning could have on the lives of millions of disadvantaged people in Asia and Africa.

೧ઌ

In a private gathering in Delhi in 2011, the Dalai Lama again talked to Abed and Davis about educating the heart. This time, he chose to focus on the importance of fostering self-confidence among the poor and how that could contribute to the flourishing of their communities.

"When I met some poor people, I think helping their self-confidence very important," the Dalai Lama said. "They often feel frustration, and their frustration sometimes transform into anger. So that's no good. More self-confidence helps them work hard, then more successful society, more successful family. We have to show respect, then help."

He pulled himself ramrod straight in his chair, thrust his chin forward, and looked up at the ceiling. "The way to help, not looking like this," he said as he mimicked someone with an over-developed sense of hauteur. "They also same human being so we must respect. That shows them we are all equal. Then these people get more enthusiastic, more ready to study, to train, to work hard, then success come. Some kind of inferior feeling is big source of problem."

He paused and remained silent for a long moment. Then his face lit up as he remembered an incident. "Oh, one example, one time in South Africa, Soweto. One time I visited there, I requested to people who arranged my visit: I want to see one ordinary family in Soweto. Finally they arrange. While talking with mother and few children, another relative came, a teacher of school. I told him: Now you already achieve democracy on paper, but mind, mental level, it takes longer time to transform, to achieve real equality. Then that teacher told me"—the Dalai Lama lowered his voice to a conspiratorial whisper—"he believes the native African brain little inferior."

He paused again, his face a picture of melancholy.

"Then I really felt very, very sad," he said. "I argued this is totally wrong. I made some comparison: We Tibetans also similar situation, sometimes some hard-liner Han Chinese people, they believe Tibetan people backwards. So I mentioned that when we have same opportunity we also become equal. We have basically same brain, scientifically same brain. We have same ability, same potential. Then that teacher finally, with long sigh, I don't know what . . ."

The Dalai Lama was uncertain if "sigh" was the right word. To make sure everyone knew what he meant, he exhaled loudly through his mouth, and said, "Sigh . . . like that. Then the teacher whispered to me: Now he convinced we are same human, same potential. That moment I felt tremendous relief."

The Dalai Lama's heartfelt satisfaction with what he had accomplished was palpable as he related this story.

"At least one person's thinking changed," he continued. "That we need. Sometime when I meet poorer section of people they feel discouraged and they feel they cannot do much. We need not only education but show them our respect, sincere concern. That we are equal. This I feel. Besides that, I don't know. My little experience when I met that South African I very much impressed. I think from that family, two or three children, I offered sponsorship. Still now they ask me some money for their further education, so I again supply." He laughed heartily. The thought of someone asking him, a Tibetan Buddhist monk not known for the size of his wallet, for money struck him as funny.

When I heard the story, two things made an impression on me. As the Dalai Lama travels the globe, he regularly lectures large audiences. Security concerns and the imperatives of these large-scale events often prevent him from interacting with people on Main Street. So he finds it particularly meaningful when he gets an opportunity to sit down with ordinary folks like the impoverished family in Soweto. And the encounter took on an added dimension when the Dalai Lama was able, through his personal intervention, to make a difference in their lives. That one transformative moment at a humble abode in Soweto would stay in the Dalai Lama's memory. And he would tell that story regularly.

I have heard the Dalai Lama talk about educating the heart many times, mostly in Western countries. He cautions his audiences not to focus all their energies on obtaining multiple advanced degrees and accumulating wealth. He hopes that they will also acquire the capacity to do the right thing, to cultivate a "warm heart." This message certainly falls on fertile ground in

North America and Europe. But to me a variation of this message is relevant in developing countries as well, especially in war-ravaged states, where people have always lived with unrelenting poverty, violence, and precious little self-esteem or trust.

In South Africa, the Dalai Lama managed to touch a few lives in a single family. He derived a great deal of satisfaction knowing that he was able to shore up their self-confidence and fire up their enthusiasm to do something worthwhile with their lives. The Dalai Lama has no doubt that educating the heart is a universal message that is relevant in many parts of the world.

Part Three

COMPASSION
IN ACTION

*It is not enough to be compassionate. You must act. There are
two aspects to action. One is to overcome the distortions and
afflictions of your own mind, that is, in terms of calming and
eventually dispelling anger. This is action out of compassion.
The other is more social, more public. When something needs
to be done in the world to rectify the wrongs, if one is really
concerned with benefiting others, one needs to be engaged,
involved.*

—His Holiness the Dalai Lama

MONKS IN
THE MACHINE

The Dalai Lama stood relaxed yet attentive in the Keck Laboratory for Biological Imaging at the University of Wisconsin–Madison in 2001. His arms were uncharacteristically clasped behind his back and his head slightly cocked to one side. He was listening very carefully to what Professor Richard Davidson was telling him about the nuts and bolts of state-of-the-art brain imaging. Making sense of the flickering images displayed in the banks of computers before him could not have been an easy task for a man who has never taken a class in Biology 101, and who, for the past seven decades, has immersed himself totally in spiritual attainment.

However, the Dalai Lama wholeheartedly believes that Buddhism and science have much in common. Both seek to explain reality as accurately as possible, albeit from different perspectives. For much of his life, the Dalai Lama has had great admiration for the scientific method. And he has said that he would have no qualms about abandoning any of his long-held Buddhist beliefs if science could prove them to be false.

Davidson pointed to a computer where several colorful pulsing graphics were displayed. "This shows the brain of someone who has been looking at photos of happy babies and smiling people. You can see that there is a lot of activity in this area known as the left prefrontal cortex, right here. This is the area that lights up when people report that they are in a good mood, energetic. Essentially when they are happy." He pointed at his own left temple to show approximately where the region is located.

"But energetic can be a negative thing," the Dalai Lama said.

"That's true. This is one of the questions that we hope you'll help us think through in our research," Davidson replied.

The two made their way through a tight throng of scientists, graduate students, and half a dozen men with heavy professional video equipment. A mini-forest of microphones mounted on overhead booms hovered above their heads. Their progress was slow and awkward; the State Department security agents assigned to protect the Dalai Lama were happy to remain low-key in the unfamiliar environs of a high-technology laboratory. Davidson and the Dalai Lama paid little attention to the crowd around them and were deeply focused on their conversation.

Davidson—named one of *Time*'s one hundred most influential people in the world in 2006—led the Dalai Lama into another section of the lab. A large window set into one wall looked out onto a room housing the large, tanklike functional magnetic resonance imaging (fMRI) machine that generates the colorful computer images of the brain. A woman was lying in its tube-like cavity.

"Your Holiness," Davidson said, "we will now show you how we use the fMRI to explore the functions of the brain. We are looking for changes in neural circuits that are produced by physical movement. We are going to ask Chris to tap her fingers. We should then see changes on the monitor showing activation in the part of the brain that controls hand movement."

The fMRI started up and a loud, discordant, clanging sound could be heard. Davidson's assistant manning the controls spoke into a microphone, "Chris, begin tapping." Davidson gently steered the Dalai Lama closer to the monitor. Peeking through a gap between them, I could see distinct spots of color materializing within an oval confine—the computer-generated outline of the brain. After a minute or so, the assistant asked Chris to stop and the spots receded.

The Dalai Lama's next question surprised Davidson. The Tibetan wanted to know what would happen if, instead of moving her fingers physically, Chris did so only mentally. The neuroscientist conferred with his colleague and made the necessary changes in the experiment protocol.

"We will now ask Chris to tap her fingers purely in her mind," he said to the Dalai Lama. "Then we will see whether we can see similar changes in her brain. This is pure experiment."

His assistant again spoke into his mike, "Chris, we will start the next paradigm. You doing okay?"

"I'm fine," Chris said.

"The instructions will be the same. When I say 'Tap,' you imagine tapping. And when I say 'No tap,' stop."

Sure enough, as Chris held the thought of moving fingers in her mind, the color spots reappeared on the monitor. But I noticed that there were now more of them and they were more evenly distributed within the oval.

"Your Holiness," Davidson said, pleased with the results. "This is the first time we have been able to do this, to be able to see changes in the brain as someone is experiencing something that is totally imaginary."

"But do thoughts come first, then change takes place in brain?" the Dalai Lama wanted to know.

"This is an important question," Davidson answered. "Our technique currently is too imprecise to answer your question. There is a delay of a few seconds, caused by the time lag in blood flow. So we are only able to see the changes in the brain after the thought has started."

There was an easy give-and-take between the American scientist and the Tibetan monk. Davidson told me later that he had been impressed that the Dalai Lama was so inquisitive and analytical.

The Dalai Lama has always had a keen scientific mind. When he was a young boy, he often tried to repair the generator in his summer palace, which tended to break down frequently. That was how he learned about internal-combustion engines. And how he discovered that a magnetic field was created when the dynamo turned on its own.

At the time, there were three motor cars in all of Lhasa. They had been taken apart and carried over the mountains on the backs of porters and then reassembled. There were two 1927 Baby Austins, one blue and the other red and yellow, and also a large orange Dodge from 1931. They had not been used since the death of the Thirteenth Dalai Lama, and had rusted badly. The young Dalai Lama managed, with the help of a young Tibetan who had been trained as a driver in India, to get two of them to work again. Those were thrilling moments for the monk and budding scientist.

The Dalai Lama and Davidson had first met in Dharamsala in 1992. Davidson had become fascinated with meditation while he was a graduate student in the 1960s. He traveled to India for spiritual retreats. Davidson told me that his first meeting with the Dalai Lama proved to be an emotional roller coaster. For some unknown reason, he had been extraordinarily anxious before he walked into the audience room.

"I was extremely nervous. I nearly had a panic attack," Davidson said. Having known him for more than ten years now, I find this puzzling. He is one of the most self-confident persons I've met; no doubt a consequence of his superlative academic accomplishments.

"I didn't know what I was going to say to the Dalai Lama," Davidson told me. "I also began to doubt myself. Why am I here, who am I to waste his time? But then, within fifteen seconds of my being in his presence, every smidgen of anxiety dissipated. I sensed and was in awe of his extraordinary power of compassion. I went from being very anxious to having a feeling of profound security. It happened just like that." He snapped his fingers.

The Dalai Lama knew that his visitor was a renowned psychologist and brain scientist. He challenged him to use his skills to study positive qualities such as kindness and compassion with the same zest that he applied to his research of depression, anxiety, and fear.

Davidson was a changed man that day in 1992. He made a solemn commitment to the Dalai Lama and himself. He would do everything in his power to put compassion on the scientific map.

Nineteen years later, a day after the Keck Laboratory visit, Davidson briefed the Dalai Lama on a study that had been concluded only a few hours earlier. "We are specifically trying to understand what the brain is showing during the expression of compassion. We want to know how that might help us to better activate those parts of the brain instrumental in cultivating compassion," he said.

The Dalai Lama responded without a beat, and with a straight face, "Through injection. That's the easiest."

Davidson and everyone around him cracked up.

"We've learned that there are mental practices that can change the brain, and that they may be the most effective ways of producing permanent change," Davidson continued with his train of thought. "Your Holiness, we scanned your French translator Matthieu Ricard's brain the day before you arrived in Madison. My students and staff worked almost the whole night analyzing his data so that I could tell you about it."

Davidson began by projecting a slide onto the large overhead screen. It showed a middle-aged Westerner wearing the maroon robes of a Tibetan monk, lying prone on a metal gurney. Matthieu Ricard, a bestselling author and longtime student of Tibetan Buddhism, was about to be slotted into the cavity of a state-of-the-art fMRI scanner. Ricard had his arms raised toward the ceiling, as if trying to stop himself from being propelled forward into the dark maw.

The Dalai Lama, seated in the lotus position on an armchair next to Davidson, threw his arms up in the air to mimic a panicking Ricard. He laughed heartily at his own joke.

The next slide showed Ricard sitting on the gurney and smiling beatifically at a standing Davidson. "Matthieu was in the brain scanner for more than three hours, and we have never, ever had a person before who came out of there smiling," Davidson reported.

The Dalai Lama said something in Tibetan. Thupten Jinpa, his Montreal-based translator, repeated the words in English to the assembled group. "His Holiness said that probably half of that could be attributed to him being French. The difference in culture—his being a very advanced culture—played a role here." Jinpa was laughing uncontrollably; he had trouble looking away from a smiling Ricard, an old friend, who sat across the table from him.

The third slide showed the French monk undergoing a different study. His bald pate and the upper part of his face were covered with something that looked like a shower cap made of thick mesh. Embedded in the mesh were hundreds of electrodes that resembled miniature hair curlers.

The Dalai Lama was captivated by these unusual—and, to him, hilarious—images of Ricard. His shoulders jiggled up and down with mirth. He has known the Frenchman for decades and is very fond of the monk, respecting him highly as a serious practitioner.

Davidson explained that the network of 256 electrodes encircling Ricard's scalp was connected to a bank of computers. Each electrode measured the infinitesimal electrical outbursts from a tiny sliver of brain. Using sophisticated triangulation techniques, the electrodes provided a detailed, three-dimensional picture of Ricard's brain in different emotional states. At the time, in 2001, only three or four labs in the world had the capacity to localize electrical impulses from the brain with such precision.

"Your Holiness, as you know, we have been studying compassion for some time," Davidson said to the Dalai Lama, who was swaying gently from side to side in his chair, as is his habit. "You have told us over the years of the importance of compassion in everyday life. But it is something that has hardly been studied by Western scientists at all. Here in our lab, we asked Matthieu to meditate on compassion, and his data would be compared with that of laypeople. We wanted to see if any feature of Matthieu's brain had changed. Just before lunch today, one of my postdoctoral fellows handed me the data. He was up most of the night analyzing it. The next slide will show you one important finding."

The slide depicted a simple graph. Within its vertical and horizontal coordinates, many data points were joined together to form the crude outline of a mountain that represented readings collected from 150 university students who had gone through the same brain scanner. Way to the left of the mountain, close to the baseline juncture of the coordinates, was one isolated, lone dot: Ricard's.

In this study, Davidson was particularly interested in an electrical signal known as "gamma," which is generated in the left prefrontal cortex of the brain. His research has shown that a high output of gamma is associated with heightened feelings of happiness. People who generate a lot of gamma tend to be joyful and optimistic. Most of the 150 students had results clustered around the central chunk of the mountain. Their emotional states were neutral most of the time—neither too happy nor too depressed. The readings that fell along the left shoulder of the mountain were from people who tend to have a consistently sunny outlook on life; those on the right shoulder came from individuals who tend to be depressed.

Ricard's number, however, nearly fell off the chart. His outlier data showed that joy and fulfillment permeate his entire consciousness. He entered into a state of euphoria when he meditated on compassion. Ricard explained, "It's a compassion that has no agenda, a compassion that excludes no one. You generate this sense of loving, and you let it soak the mind. You focus on the wish that all sentient beings be free from suffering."

An excited Richardson said to the Dalai Lama, "These are some of the first data that we're aware of—looking at brain activity during the focused generation of compassion."

After the Dalai Lama left Madison and returned to India, Davidson continued to research the relationship between compassion meditation and brain function, and, in particular, how our mental processes—thoughts, emotions, meditation—could alter the physical structure and function of our brains. With the help of the Dalai Lama and Ricard, he invited eight Tibetan Buddhist monks to visit the Keck lab. Davidson scanned their brains while they meditated on compassion. Periodically, he also exposed them to sounds of intense human suffering: a woman screaming or a baby crying inconsolably.

The monks had meditated an average of 34,000 hours each in their lifetimes; some of them had meditated for as many as 64,000 hours. And everyone had completed at least one three-year solitary retreat. Davidson recruited ten college students, who were given a crash course in meditation, as a control group.

The results were striking. Most of the meditating monks showed very large increases in gamma waves in their left prefrontal cortex—a clear sign that they were experiencing intense periods of well-being. The signals produced were thirty times as powerful as those of the students. A few monks—those with the most hours of meditation—showed "extremely large increases of the sort that have never been reported before in the neuro-science literature," according to Davidson.

After seeing these results, Davidson was excited by the prospect that structural brain changes could possibly be induced by mental training. And that we can intentionally cultivate positive traits such as empathy and kindness. He envisions something like going to the gym to develop a more efficient cardiovascular system—a mental exercise routine for fostering a deeply compassionate state of mind, and an effective antidote to afflictions like anxiety and depression.

❧

These results must have been very gratifying for the Dalai Lama. His seven decades (and counting) of spiritual practices have produced a simple insight: Altruism is the surest and most effective way to bring about genuine life satisfaction. He did not arrive at this intellectually—he experienced it through his own practice.

There is a good reason why the Dalai Lama has frequently sought out the company of illustrious scientists. He knows that simple techniques like meditation are good for us. He believes that they systematically enhance our sense of compassion and contentment, and are effective in reducing mental anguish. The Dalai Lama had hoped science would one day validate this understanding. And now there was neurological evidence, in the laboratory of Richard Davidson, and a growing body of psychological research that corroborated the valuable effects of meditation. Science has confirmed that the more altruistic we become, the happier we are.

As dramatic as these results were, they were not, based on earlier studies, entirely unexpected. However, Davidson was taken aback by one finding. Although the monks were perfectly still in the scanner during their meditation on compassion, the motor regions of their brains—the motor cortex and the basal ganglia—were unusually active. These areas are linked to the intention to act, and their activation often precedes voluntary action. The research team thought initially that these findings might be due to noise artifacts in the instrumentation. But they found the same puzzling results after they had fine-tuned the scanner.

The monks themselves did not find the results surprising. Matthieu Ricard told Davidson that these findings were consistent with what he believes is a key aspect of compassion. The area of the brain associated with action was triggered during compassion meditation. It prepped the mind to move into high gear, to provide help as soon as suffering was encountered. The thought processes that were involved proved to be quick and automatic. Whatever barrier there was between self and others was dissolved. Those who are compassionate—through training or by nature—are hardwired to help those in distress. Logic and common sense have little say in the matter, as demonstrated when Wesley Autrey was compelled to jump down onto a New York City subway track and lie on top of a stranger who had fallen in during a seizure, saving him from a train passing over them.

I have often wondered why a Buddhist monk like the Dalai

Lama is so involved in science. For nearly three decades, he has had frequent and regular conversations with scientists of all stripes—physicists, psychologists, geneticists, neuroscientists. This cross-fertilization of science and Buddhism is serendipitous. Advances in science, like those that came out of Davidson's laboratory, validate the efficacy of a 2,500-year-old body of knowledge designed to root out the causes of suffering. These days, we all pay a great deal of attention to science, especially to those findings that could have an impact on our mental well-being and physical health. The Dalai Lama is gratified that science has convincingly demonstrated key aspects of his worldview—the intimate correlation between compassion and action, and how they together help lead us to authentic happiness and a meaningful life.

A BOY FROM DOON

When social activist and educator Sanjit "Bunker" Roy sat down with the Dalai Lama for the first time, he had a confession to make: "Your Holiness, I got a very snobbish, elitist, and expensive education in India. I went to the Doon School."

They were in Zurich, attending the 2010 conference "Altruism and Compassion in Economic Systems," sponsored by the Mind & Life Institute. Roy, a silver-haired Indian in his sixties, was dressed simply in a maroon kurta—a knee-length, open-necked shirt—and white cotton trousers. I thought perhaps he had consciously chosen the color of his attire to echo that of the Dalai Lama's robes. Roy, while distinguished-looking, did not appear to be all that different from many well-educated, well-to-do middle-class Indians I've met over the years in India. Except perhaps for one small detail: he wore a watch on each wrist.

"When I was a very young boy, you came to Doon with the Panchen Lama," Roy told the Dalai Lama. Doon, modeled after

Britain's Eton and Harrow, is the school of choice for India's business and power elite.

"Yes, in 1956," the Dalai Lama replied immediately. I was not surprised that he remembered this rather obscure visit that took place more than half a century earlier. I have often seen breathtaking demonstrations of his prodigious memory.

But the Dalai Lama also had very good reasons to remember 1956. It was his first visit to India, the land that gave birth to Buddhism. In 1951, Mao Zedong had turned his attention to Tibet, and by 1956, his armies were making alarming progress in their advance toward Lhasa. The Dalai Lama took advantage of an invitation to celebrate the 2,500th anniversary of the Buddha's birth and went on a pilgrimage to India. While in Delhi, he asked Jawaharlal Nehru, then prime minister, for asylum. Nehru, however, was working hard to improve Sino-Indian relations and declined the request. The Dalai Lama returned to Tibet with a strong sense of foreboding.

"Your Holiness, you know what Indians are like," Roy said. "My future was all laid out for me by my family. The jobs were all laid out. Doctor, engineer, or diplomat. But then there was the Bihar famine of 1966. I went there to help."

In the summer of 1966, ten years after that initial encounter between Roy and the Dalai Lama, India's eastern province of Bihar experienced one of the worst and most widespread droughts and crop failures in history. Massive local, national, and international relief efforts were mobilized to prevent death by starvation on an immense scale.

"Working in Bihar changed my life," Roy said. "When I came

home, I told my mother that I wanted to live and work in a village. My mother went into a coma . . ."

The Dalai Lama didn't know the word, and his translator, Thupten Jinpa, explained. Then he bent down, untied his shoelaces, removed his shoes, and folded his legs lotus-style on the armchair. He was enjoying himself and wanted to be as comfortable as possible.

Roy continued, "After my mother recovered from the shock, she asked, 'What do you want to do in a village?' I said that I want to be an unskilled laborer, digging wells. That upset her even more. She didn't speak to me for six months. I had brought the image of the family down. I have been working in a village for the last forty years. Your Holiness, elite education makes us arrogant, conceited. It makes us think we are the answers to everything. You know what this expensive education does to us? It destroys us."

The Dalai Lama was captivated by the Indian's matter-of-fact but provocative delivery and was trying hard not to laugh out loud. He was hugely entertained by Roy's unconventional pronouncements but perhaps deemed it impolitic to encourage him.

"For five years I dug wells as an unskilled laborer," Roy continued. "And that was when I was exposed to the most extraordinary skills, knowledge, and wisdom that very poor people have. It does not come from books, from universities; you don't read about it, you have to feel it. I thought that this knowledge needed to be brought into the mainstream, and that was when I started the Barefoot College in a small village. A poor man in the village told me that there was something I must not do. I said,

'What is that?' He said, 'Please don't bring anyone with a degree into your college.' So anyone with a Ph.D. or a M.Sc. is disqualified. It has to be someone working with his hands."

The Dalai Lama nodded vigorously. I could see that the idea of the dignity of labor, the dignity of the poor, resonated strongly with him. The Dalai Lama has always had a soft spot for the disadvantaged. I believe he got this from his mother. She was famous for lavishing affection not only on her family but also on all others who came into contact with her. If she saw poor Tibetans in the street, she would often invite them into her home and give them food or money. She kept large boxes of rice and wheat in the house, and people would come to the back door to ask for food.

The Dalai Lama has always identified with the underdog. He used to keep an air rifle when he lived in Lhasa. He showed it to me when I visited his home in Dharamsala, India. He told me, "I often feed small birds, but when they come together, hawks spot them and catch them. Very bad. So to protect these small birds, I keep air rifle to scare them away. A compassionate rifle!"

Roy continued his story about the Barefoot College. "We believe in the lifestyle of Gandhi. We sit on the floor, eat on the floor, work on the floor. And no one gets more than $100 a month. Ever. Because you don't come for the money. You come for the challenge and you come to work with the poor."

The Dalai Lama was sitting in an unusual manner. He leaned far to the left of his chair so that his back was resting uncomfortably against the wooden armrest. He wanted to be in a better position to observe Roy.

"At the college we foster the capacity of the poor," Roy said. "We give them the opportunity to develop themselves. It is the only college built by someone who still cannot read or write. He built it at $1.50 a square foot. We believe we can bring in the most sophisticated technology but not at the expense of traditional wisdom and know-how. It is the only college in India that is fully solar-energized. All our computers, telephone exchange, cooking work off the sun. It was installed by a Hindu priest who had only eight years of schooling."

Roy was in his element. His expressive hands, moving in concert with his words, described large slashes in the air. He started to speak louder, his voice reaching a minor crescendo, "We said: Where is it written that just because you can't read or write you can't become an architect, a dentist, an engineer?"

He sat at the edge of his chair and held out his hands to the Dalai Lama in an exaggerated gesture of supplication. I thought for a moment that he was about to kneel down on the floor before him. "Your Holiness, do you agree? You agree?"

The Dalai Lama nodded obediently. He and Jinpa glanced at each other and started to laugh. They were swept along by the animal energy and passion of Roy.

The Dalai Lama likes to laugh. He laughs more than most people I know. It seems to be in his family's genes. The Dalai Lama and Tenzin Choegyal, his youngest brother, are very similar. Both are prone to frequent, explosive, body-shaking laughter. They are also fond of cracking dirty jokes, at least in private. In his youth, the Dalai Lama had a religious assistant who always told him, "If you can really laugh with full abandonment, it's very good for your health."

After the laughter subsided, Bunker Roy said, "We take people from the village who never had any formal education. We train them to be teachers, doctors, engineers, computer experts. We have a grandmother who does not know how to read or write but we trained her to perform a root canal."

Barefoot College has trained hundreds of semiliterate and illiterate grandmothers from developing countries to be solar engineers. Through that program, they have electrified more than six hundred villages in India. Some are in very remote areas in the Himalayas and can be reached only after long treks on foot.

Roy said, "We went to Ladakh's Nubra Valley, Your Holiness. As you know, it is minus forty degrees Fahrenheit there in the winter."

"Yes, yes, I know. Very cold," the Dalai Lama agreed. Ladakh is a predominantly Tibetan area in northwest India, and he goes there from time to time, but always in the summer.

"After we electrified a village in Nubra," Roy said, "I asked a Tibetan woman what she thought was the benefit of solar energy. This woman thought for a minute and told me, 'It's the first time I can see my husband's face in winter.'"

Solar power also has a huge impact on education. Since most children cannot go to school in the morning, because they have to look after the livestock, Barefoot College runs schools at night using solar lanterns.

"Your Holiness, we have seven thousand children in a hundred fifty schools," Roy said. "We believe that a child should know about citizenship and democracy. So we have an election in the schools. We have a child parliament. The children themselves elected a prime minister who is twelve years old. She looks after twenty goats in the morning. But in the evening she is prime minister. She has a cabinet that monitors and supervises their own school. And every decision the child makes we have to implement. She won the World's Children's Prize in 2007. This twelve-year-old had never left her village in her life, but she went to Sweden to get the prize from the queen."

The Dalai Lama was impressed. The prize—the world's largest annual educational program for young people—focuses on promoting the rights of the child, democracy, the environment, and global friendship. More than fifty thousand schools with 24 million students in more than a hundred countries are involved. In a global vote, 7 million children get to decide who will receive the award.

"The queen of Sweden couldn't believe that this twelve-year-old girl was not dazzled by anything around her," Roy told the Dalai Lama. "She asked me to ask the prime minister where she got her confidence. So I asked the girl. She looked very insulted and looked straight at the queen and said, 'Please tell her I'm the prime minister.'"

The Dalai Lama has firsthand knowledge of the prize. One of his sisters, Jetsun Pema, received an award in 2006 for her forty-year struggle for the Tibetan refugee children in India. Her work has saved untold lives and given tens of thousands of children a home, education, and hope. Nearly fifteen thousand children are under her care every year.

Roy's Barefoot approach was an unqualified success in India. In recent years, he decided to go global and replicated the program in some of the least developed countries in the world, such as Ethiopia and Afghanistan. By 2006, a total of thirty-six semiliterate and illiterate villagers had been trained and had completed solar installations in nineteen Ethiopian villages. Afghanistan's Barefoot solar engineers, by the end of 2008, had electrified a hundred villages there.

"I went to the United Nations for a meeting," Roy told the Dalai Lama. "I told them we had brought three Afghan women to India. I bought the airfare, bought the equipment, trained them for six months. They went home and electrified five villages. I asked the United Nations officials, 'Guess how much it all cost?' They didn't have a clue. I told them the expenses were the same as what it costs to pay one UN consultant sitting at a desk in Kabul for one year. I told them it is scandalous that there are seven hundred consultants there and not one village has solar."

The Dalai Lama laughed.

"So, Your Holiness, we learned a very important lesson. Men are untrainable," Roy said.

The Dalai Lama conferred with Jinpa to make sure he had heard this correctly.

"Men are restless, men are ambitious," Roy elaborated. "Men are compulsively mobile and they all want a certificate. And the moment you give them a cert—"

"And you yourself?" The Dalai Lama could not resist.

"Nay, Your Holiness, I'm a lost cause."

"Wonderful. Really wonderful," the Dalai Lama told Roy, with feeling.

"The moment you give them a certificate they will leave the village in one day and look for a job in the city."

"Yes, yes, that's right."

"So for me the best investments are grandmothers. The best. The grandmothers, between forty and fifty, are the most mature, most tolerant. I have women from all over Africa. They have never been outside their village. I fly them to India for training. Through sign language, without the written word, without the spoken word, we train them to be solar engineers. They come as grandmothers, they go back as tigers. So, Your Holiness, if you have a grandmother that you would like to send to the Barefoot College, we'd be delighted. I have a quote from Gandhi: 'First they ignore you, then they laugh at you, then they fight you. And then you win.'"

Roy put his palms together at chest level, stood up, and bowed. He was finished. The Dalai Lama started to applaud. It was a gentle clapping, his hands coming together ever so lightly, without much force and not at all loud. Clapping was not his thing. I have seldom seen him do this.

"Really wonderful," he said solemnly to Roy. "I have conviction that the real transformation of India must start from the countryside, from the village. Your method wonderful, I really appreciate. In the meantime, I want some of your illiterate teachers come to our settlement. Our young Tibetans also very eager for some certificate and they usually go big cities for jobs. Big problem for our settlements. So I really want to invite you, when you have some time."

The Dalai Lama put his palms in front of his face and inclined his head as he made his request.

"Your Holiness, for you, anytime," Roy said with a big smile.

"So perhaps you go and give encouragement to our older generation, many of them illiterate. I think eventually the Chinese also should learn your method. Their coastal area much developed, but the interior very poor. Teach them how to develop, how to transform. Not from Karl Marx." The Dalai Lama pointed a finger at Roy and said loudly, "You Indian guru. Wonderful, wonderful!"

This was classic Dalai Lama. He was sold on Roy's innovative, unconventional, and apparently very effective methods to improve the lives of the poor. He very much wanted him to help his fellow Tibetans. But at the same time, the welfare of the Chinese, most of whom are known to have an unsympathetic view of him, was front and center in his mind as well.

A BEAUTIFUL
DALAI LAMA

It was January 8, 2011, the coldest day of the year for New Delhi. The temperature was a whopping nine degrees Fahrenheit below normal. There had been at least three cold-related deaths, and schools were closed indefinitely. Dense fog shrouded the city, and visibility had dropped to fifty feet. It was nine-thirty in the morning. It might as well have been nine-thirty at night.

The Taj Palace Hotel's Mumtaz Mahal Hall was brightly lit. Decked with impossibly intricate wall hangings, thick carpeting, and a few too many chandeliers, it was like any number of five-star hotel conference rooms in the Indian capital. Opulent, yes, but also generic, a touch sterile.

The Dalai Lama had just arrived and taken a seat in front of forty-four invited guests and their spouses from four continents and one subcontinent. They were a small assembly of CEOs, writers, social entrepreneurs, and philanthropists with one thing in common: they channeled outsized passion and resources into alleviating suffering among the extreme poor. They were gathered here to tell the Dalai Lama about their work and, hopefully, get some nuggets of wisdom and inspiration from him.

At the start of the session, I stood on a small stage, holding a microphone, and told the Dalai Lama, "Your Holiness, I'd like to begin today's meeting by talking about magic. But I think you are not going to be very pleased about this."

The Dalai Lama, sitting in the armchair next to me, was preoccupied with adjusting his robes, and making sure that his lapel mike was attached properly. He did not look at me and showed no reaction to what I had said.

I plunged ahead. "I'm quite sure I was the first long-haired Chinese hippie to meet you in your home in Dharamsala, thirty-nine years ago."

There was a smattering of titters in the room.

"It was a life-transforming experience for me," I continued. "Before that, I was on track to become rich and famous, thanks to the formidable will of my mother. But after meeting you, I have acquired neither fame nor riches. However, I believe I lead a fulfilling life, thanks to having listened to your teachings and having learned from you for many years. So this is the magic I am talking about. I know that you have always insisted that you have no special powers, and certainly no magic. Well, in my case, I don't think this is quite true."

I glanced at the Dalai Lama. He sat in his chair, like a sphinx, I thought. He looked straight ahead at the small group and there was a total lack of expression on his face. It was disconcerting.

Nonplussed, I turned to speak to the group, my words coming out faster than I had intended: "All of you are accomplished humanitarians. You work with people in extreme poverty. You are highly motivated and you have great passion. When all of you come together in a small room like this, and in the presence of His Holiness, I hope something magical, something transformative will indeed happen."

The room was a touch too cool; perhaps the hotel heating system had trouble coping with the unseasonably cold temperature outside. The Dalai Lama had carefully wrapped his maroon outer shawl around his upper torso so that the golden lapels of his shirt were concealed. He sat in the lotus position, his legs folded neatly on top of the cushion of his chair, his hands resting lightly on his knees. I noticed that both of his thumbs flicked rhythmically and unobtrusively against his forefingers. It was as if he were holding two strings of imaginary prayer beads in his hands and cycling methodically through each of their 108 beads as he mentally repeated a mantra. Even in a setting like a hotel conference room, he didn't miss an opportunity to practice mindfulness.

"I'm extremely happy to be with you who dedicated to the well-being of others, the needy people," the Dalai Lama told the small group, his upper body swaying gently from side to side. "I can express gratitude on behalf of those millions of people who not much think about wider things but simply concern their daily lives, 'If I consume this piece of bread, then at the time of dinner what I should eat?' They are not able to appeal to other people for help, they simply carrying their day-by-day suffering."

Without taking his eyes off the group, he extended an arm toward me and said, "He mentioned something about magic. It is quite clear: he is long time my friend, so naturally he has to praise, so don't believe what he says."

I was relieved that he did not rebuke me in front of everyone about the use of the word "magic" in talking about him. Ever since I have known him, he has shown a deep aversion to the idea, fervently advanced by some of his ardent followers, that he has any special powers. His lifelong mission is to help us awaken our innate capacity for compassion and thus live a meaningful life. The last thing he wants us to do is to cling to the idea that he possesses supernatural power that could magically help solve our problems. For him, the only real "magic" comes from discipline, responsibility, wisdom, and altruism. For some years, the Dalai Lama had been plagued with an enlarged gallbladder. He finally had it removed in a Delhi hospital a few years ago. He had described his ailment to me in some detail and then said with great satisfaction, "Some people believe that I have magical powers. If I have this power, then I would use it on myself to cure my gallbladder problem. So now there is scientific proof that I am just an ordinary person."

The Dalai Lama had agreed to spend an entire day at this meeting in Delhi, providing the gravitas and moral authority to help us focus on improving the lives of the very poor. He has this uncanny ability to bring out the best in people. I have no doubt that our ethical behavior and commitment to the greater good are often enhanced in his presence. We are also inspired to carefully examine and repurpose our motivations. A key challenge for me was to bring the right combination of individuals to the table. It was important to have a diversity of perspectives and experience. To foster a focused and in-depth dialogue, I tried to keep the numbers small. To ensure good communication and collaboration, I sought out those who were likely to leave their considerable egos at the door.

One of the attendees was Zainab Salbi, a slim, fine-boned woman with dark hair cut so short that she could be mistaken for a nun—if not for her fashionable outfit. Her well-fitting black dress and chic black jacket were nicely set off by a long, colorful scarf that she had looped a couple of times around her neck. I beckoned to her and she strode up to the stage.

"I'd like to introduce you to my friend Zainab, whom I nearly succeeded in bringing to Vancouver in 2009 to meet you," I said to the Dalai Lama. "But at the last minute, because of her fortieth-birthday celebrations, she could not come."

"She is from——?" the Dalai Lama asked.

"She is from Iraq," I replied.

Salbi stood ramrod straight a few steps from the Dalai Lama. She held a folder of notes, an expectant smile lighting up her expressive face.

"In 1993, Zainab founded an organization called Women for Women," I said. "Since that time, her efforts have had an impact on 270,000 women in war zones, and she has given about ninety million dollars in direct aid and loans, mostly to poor women in Africa and the Middle East."

Of the 35 million people who are driven from their homes

by conflicts around the world, most are women and children. Women are often victims of ethnic cleansing, rape, and other horrendous crimes. If they manage to survive, they are the ones who shoulder the thankless tasks of rebuilding daily life in a post-conflict society. They are the invisible and unsung heroes. They are little noticed and their voices remain unheard amid the cacophony of urgent military, security, and geopolitical issues.

Salbi's organization helps women recover from the trauma of war. It shepherds them into a semblance of normalcy by giving them direct aid, job training, microfinance, and education. She herself grew up in relative comfort and privilege. Her father was Saddam Hussein's personal pilot, and her family socialized regularly with Hussein and his inner circle. Salbi's mother was a powerful influence and instilled in her the importance of education. She followed her mother's advice and rebelled against assuming the traditional female role in Iraqi society. She never learned how to cook or clean the house.

Salbi walked up to the Dalai Lama, bent low from the waist, and held both his hands for a moment before sitting down beside him. She touched her right hand to her chest while the Dalai Lama greeted her in a traditional palms-together Buddhist gesture.

"Your Holiness," Salbi said. "Because I grew up in war and then worked in war I learned I had better enjoy life while I can. So I wanted to celebrate my fortieth birthday and dance. I trust that you'd know that and understand the need to celebrate the joyfulness of life."

The Dalai Lama nodded and took her hand in his. But he did not reply.

The Dalai Lama has a singular take on birthdays. I'd heard him explain his view this way: "Usually I don't consider birthdays something important. In our tradition we consider the death anniversary more important. I think that's quite wise. A person who made good contributions in life, then after his death, remember him in some anniversaries, that's good. But birthdays, with much celebrations, then later that person becomes negative, not much meaning. I already in my seventies, so I don't think there is much danger I become negative. As a Buddhist monk I believe every day is new day, every day is birthday. The particles of our bodies momentarily changing, always become something new. Mental thinking, because of new experiences, new knowledge, also changes. So every day is birthday. The important thing is: We should utilize our every new day proper way. Then days, months, decades, whole life becomes meaningful. If you can help other, do it as much as you can. If you cannot, at least restrain harming others. That's the essential of meaningful life."

Salbi began to tell the Dalai Lama about the plight suffered by women: two-thirds of the poorest people in the world are women; women constitute 80 percent of all refugees; one woman in four is abused and violently beaten at some time in her life; trafficking of women and children is the third-largest illegal trade in the world, after arms and drugs.

"Yet we are not outraged by it," she said to the Dalai Lama, staring at him intently. "We are numb to the violence and injustice against women. We cannot continue like this. I appeal particularly to Your Holiness to help awaken our moral responsibilities, our consciousness. I was in Iraq a couple of months ago. An Iraqi sheikh told me that women are like a bird with a broken wing: it can never fly if one of its wings is broken. It is the same for a country or humanity at large. So my hope is that we create the same awakening that ended slavery, the awakening that ended apartheid. We need an awakening that ends marginalization and discrimination of women and girls."

The Dalai Lama adjusted his lapel mike, made sure that it was attached properly to the folds of his robe, cleared his throat, and said, "Yes, it's problem." He was gazing at the floor, his voice unusually subdued. He sat very still; he seemed overwhelmed by the challenges faced by women in the developing world. "I always tell people," he continued, "I have certain amount of compassion since my childhood, this actually learned from my mother, not from father. My father, like me, quite short-tempered. But my mother very, very kind. This does not come through teachings or faith. It is biological factor."

The Dalai Lama's hands rested on top of his monk's bag on his lap. His body began to sway gently from side to side. He was beginning to transition into his usual rhythm—entering a state of mindful purpose.

"Mere education is not sufficient," he said. He was no longer looking at the floor but at the audience, his voice packing noticeably more decibels and power.

He wagged a finger as he continued: "Warm heart and compassion more important. Some scientists told me that when two persons, male and female, watching someone who experiences pain, the response stronger from female—more sensitive about other's pain. Therefore, female should take more active role regarding promotion of human compassion.

"But some male chauvinist disagree with my view. But I really feel like that . . . that females more compassionate. I think sometime the word 'hero' may not be nice. Hero no hesitation to kill people. Most of these heroes male, they really merciless."

The Dalai Lama paused, lost in thought. "Oh, one time in Paris," he said, brightening, "one lady reporter asked me whether future Dalai Lama could be woman. And I said, 'Oh yes, this is actually my view, if female Dalai Lama more useful, then why not?' Then I added little joke: In case next Dalai Lama is woman, then she should be more beautiful."

All of us cracked up at this. As if he needed to provide a rationale for this heretic thought, he added, "To enthuse more people."

Another one of the participants, Ruchira Gupta, a youthful-looking Indian woman with thick glasses, stood up and said to the Dalai Lama, "Yesterday I telephoned one of the survivors of prostitution I work with. This woman lives in a small village in Bihar. At one time she had to force her way into a brothel to rescue her daughter. I told her, 'I'm going to meet the Dalai Lama, is there anything you want me to ask him?' She said, 'Who is he?' I said, 'He is a Buddhist and he believes in *ahimsa*, nonviolence.' I believe that prostitution is a form of violence to the self and to others, both from male and female perspectives. The violence women can face is incredible. In India, the U.S., and Africa I've met survivor after survivor who talks about cigarette butts being stubbed out on her, bottles being shoved up her vagina, being trafficked from village to village. This former prostitute said, 'Ask the Dalai Lama how we can get men to be less violent. How do we do this?'"

Gupta is a determined former journalist who is spearheading a worldwide campaign to stop the trafficking of women. She had spent years trying to help sex slaves, most of them in their teens or younger, sold into India's vast prostitution network. She was outraged by the inhumanity and intensity of their suffering: debilitating physical trauma and disease, mind-numbing stories of drug addiction, and unspeakable atrocities committed by both pimps and customers. Her nonprofit group, Apne Aap (meaning "self-help" in Hindi), has grown from a handful of volunteers to a program of self-empowerment and skills training involving more than ten thousand women and girls, giving impoverished prostitutes a second chance at a better life. Her documentary *Selling of Innocents* received an Emmy Award.

"This century-old kind of view," the Dalai Lama said, "this aggression, very much related to physical strength, the attitude that women are weaker physically. Basic human nature is compassionate but, through education, this basic biological factor get dormant, not further developed, because no special effort made. From education side we need lots of effort, to balance intelligence with warmheartedness. Then education becomes constructive.

"But if promote intelligence only, other positive values remain standstill, then negative things like anger, hatred combined with intelligence, then intelligence become source of aggression. We have to promote basic human values like compassion to change century-old attitude toward women. But many factors involved. We cannot solve one thing through one approach. Everything interrelated. That's why people from different professions, different experiences must work together. I myself Buddhist monk, usually people consider me as . . ."

The Dalai Lama stopped speaking for a moment. He raised his hands to chest level, their fingers fluttering rapidly. He was trying hard to come up with the right words to describe himself. "Nobel laureate," he said finally. "So in that capacity I share with you my ideas about compassion, my feelings about women. That's my profession, just talk, without implementation. All of us want happy, peaceful, compassionate world. Females certainly have important role. However, you cannot ignore male. Without male no family."

Then a thought struck him, and he said, laughing with abandon, "We monks not relevant."

Gupta, a woman of some determination, persevered with the Dalai Lama: "I appeal to you to talk to world leaders. Help us reach these men so they can tell other men not to be so violent. Also not to buy sex. Tell them that cool men don't buy sex. Hopefully this will change this culture where prostitution is so normal that nobody thinks it's wrong to rape a thirteen-year-old girl."

The Dalai Lama settled back into his chair and sighed. "I think this worldwide problem difficult to change by one single person," he said evenly to Gupta. "In India, the caste system unhealthy, it discriminates male and female. I publicly express that this is outdated part of Indian culture. This culture very much connected to faith traditionally."

He leaned forward and stared at Gupta, his hands appearing out of the cocoon of his shawl, gesturing forcefully. "So in India, religious leaders must come out and speak frankly and openly. I express many occasions. One Indian friend he also working hard to change this culture. He told me he approached some spiritual leaders, verbally they agree to support. But when he asked them writing to support . . ."

The Dalai Lama recoiled theatrically back into his chair, both palms lifted to chest level as if to stop someone physically from coming close. He was pantomiming the reactions of some Indian religious leaders when urged to help break down India's entrenched caste system. "Grassroots-level movement very important," he concluded. "We cannot expect some big change from these leaders."

The Dalai Lama has always been very consistent in his role. Because of his decades-long spiritual training, he has developed a very realistic view about himself—what he is and what he is not. He understands the limitations of his upbringing and education. He is trained as a monk. He has spent thousands upon thousands of hours trying to transform his mental traits, to diminish debilitating emotions such as hatred and attachment, and to foster compassion and forgiveness. He has had no formal modern education and he did not attend any universities (although he has garnered a truckload of honorary degrees). People who come into his presence invariably have the idea that he is omnipotent, that he has answers to everything. He does not hesitate to disabuse them of this rose-tinted view. He is careful to tell them, as he did at this gathering in Delhi, that he has some capacity to talk about things he knows, but he has no real-life experience or training to bring these ideas to fruition. There is no doubt that he was in agreement with Salbi and Gupta about women. He agonizes over the indignities women have to suffer. But he did not have any specific, tangible prescriptions as to how to make the world a better place for them. Only a singular ability to inspire others to work with compassion, and to translate that compassion into action.

THE YELLOW
HOLY WHIP

I have known Matthieu Ricard for more than twenty years. We first met in Kathmandu in the mid-1980s, when he was the personal attendant of Dilgo Khyentse Rinpoche, one of the foremost meditation masters of Tibetan Buddhism and a tutor to the Dalai Lama.

Our first encounters were unremarkable, a few meetings to compare notes on our work. I was working on my pilgrimage guide, the *Tibet Handbook*. He was working to translate a Tibetan text, *The Life of Shabkar: The Autobiography of a Tibetan Yogin*, into English. Shabkar was an eighteenth-century teacher, regarded as one of the greatest yogis in the country, who went to many of the pilgrimage places described in the handbook.

Over the following years, I marveled at Ricard's transformation from a shy, scholarly monk to an extraordinarily caring and spiritual human being. There is an unmistakable aura about him now. His broad, open face exudes goodwill, even in repose. His infectious smile is something to behold. He has about him a palpable sense of contentment that effortlessly draws people to him. His admirers are legion.

When Ricard was twenty years old, he was hired as a researcher in the cellular genetics laboratory of François Jacob, a Frenchman who had just been awarded the Nobel Prize for Medicine. He worked toward his doctorate there for six years. Ricard's life took an unexpected turn in 1967, when he visited Darjeeling in northern India and there met several Tibetan teachers. He thought that they exemplified what a fulfilled human life could be. In 1972, he abandoned the investigation of genetics and moved to India to study with some of these teachers. Ricard had finally found something that gave meaning and direction to his life. He understood that achieving sustainable happiness as a way of being requires unrelenting effort in mind-training. He learned that inner peace and altruistic love are qualities that can be acquired. He shaved his head, exchanged his blue jeans for maroon robes, and became a Tibetan Buddhist monk.

"I ended up spending forty years in the Himalayas," he told me. "At first, my life was simple, very quiet, meditating and living on pennies a day." All that changed when, one day in 1979, a publisher friend called and asked if he would collaborate on a book with his father, the celebrated French philosopher Jean-François Revel. The result of ten days of dialogue in Nepal was *The Monk and the Philosopher*. It became an instant bestseller and has been translated into twenty-one languages.

"When the book with my father came out," Ricard said, "a journalist asked me about my main regret in life. I said I regretted not being able to put into action the compassion that I was trying to cultivate in my Buddhist practice. That was a transformative moment for me. I soon created a foundation, donated all the royalties to it, and began working on humanitarian projects in Asia. Now my life has become much more hectic, but I have also discovered the lasting fulfillment that comes from helping others."

❧

Ricard and I worked together to convene a meeting with the Dalai Lama and a group of humanitarians in Delhi in January 2011 on the subject of poverty alleviation. It was an initiative that resonated with him. He oversees about forty health and education projects in Tibet, Nepal, and northern India. His focus is on very remote areas, where other organizations have no presence. His foundation treats a hundred thousand patients a year and provides education for fifteen thousand children in the schools that it has built.

"Your Holiness, I'm told that most NGOs disappear within ten years," Ricard said to the Dalai Lama in the Delhi hotel. "Why? Because of human failings. The grains of sand that bring the machine to a halt. We try to help others and suddenly everything goes off track. Corruption. Lack of transparency. Ego conflicts. But for all of us here, your high ethical standard is a powerful model. We do not expect you to tell us do this, do that, or start this project. But your presence reminds us to always check our motivation, to make sure it is altruistic."

Motivation is of critical importance to the Dalai Lama. When he wakes up every morning, usually at three-thirty a.m., he devotes considerable time to "shaping his motivation." Although he is in his seventies and has accumulated countless hours of spiritual practice, he is constantly alert to the danger of not focusing his intentions in an appropriate direction. He is determined that he will hold only good thoughts in his mind, and that he will be vigilant to speak and act with altruistic intent.

"What is violence? What is nonviolence?" the Dalai Lama had once asked me in one of our interviews in Dharamsala. "Very difficult to make clear. It is related to motivation. If we have sincere motivation, with compassion and caring in our minds, even if we speak harsh words, use physical force, these actions are nonviolent. But with negative motivation, a friendly gesture using nice words and a big smile, and try to exploit others, it is the worst kind of violence. Because of the motivation."

The Dalai Lama followed the Delhi meeting, with its mission of helping the poor, with great interest. He was impressed with the humanitarian work of Matthieu Ricard. He was delighted that the French monk practiced something he considers crucial: translating a feeling of compassion into tangible action. He has often praised those who are working to make a difference in people's lives, and he urges Tibetan Buddhists to follow their example. And the Dalai Lama was particularly delighted that Ricard, in addition to his punishing schedule managing his foundation, could still keep up his spiritual practice. He nodded when Ricard told the group, "I try to keep up the strength to be of service by carving out a few months of solitary retreat every year. I try to balance contemplation and humanitarian action, strengthening the one with the other. When the desire to help comes from deep within, that's authentic engagement. Because you are deeply concerned with the welfare of others, engagement necessarily follows. And personal transformation is important. If you are able to deepen your empathy and compassion, your ability to make a difference will be stronger."

Amod Kanth, an ex-policeman from Delhi and a participant in the conference, stood up to say, "Your Holiness, I founded an organization called Prayas in 1988. We deliver alternative education to about fifty thousand street kids. And we create shelters, provide health and nutrition for marginalized children. Not so long ago, by nightfall, we always had about fifty, sixty children, lost and homeless, taken to the police station. India is the fourth largest economy in the world, yet we have forty percent of the population living in extreme poverty. We have sixty million children who are not going to school, despite the fact that we have free and compulsory education."

In 2009, the Indian Parliament passed a bill to provide universal education for all children aged six to fourteen. It was a landmark decision. India's previous unwillingness to fund universal education had contributed to staggeringly low literacy rates. Today, more than 35 percent of India's residents are still illiterate, and official figures record that 50 percent of Indian children do not go to school.

"Your Holiness," Amod asked, "what kind of guidance do you have for the voluntary organizations, the NGOs? We seek your leadership in some tangible terms."

"Leadership needs vision," the Dalai Lama replied immediately. "I have no vision. It is easy to see something lacking. But how to make change, very difficult. I'm not expert. I have no experience: how to educate, how to help the poor. I just watch from a distance. Say all the time: wonderful, wonderful, wonderful! That's all!"

The room erupted in laughter, but it was evident that the participants were disappointed. I had hoped that the Dalai Lama would talk about initiatives to make education more readily accessible to the poor. Yet I also know that the Dalai Lama has always been reluctant to make suggestions or come up with specific solutions. Some of this reluctance can be attributed to his innate humility. He believes that he does not have the necessary hands-on experience, and he does not want to talk about things he has little knowledge of.

"The way I was educated . . ." the Dalai Lama continued, a mischievous gleam in his eyes. He leaned out of his chair and I could see he was in an impish mood. "Around seven or eight, I had no interest about study. Only play."

Loud laughter filled the room again. "One thing, my mind, since young, quite sharp, can learn easily," the Dalai Lama said. "That brings laziness. So my tutor always keep one whip, a yellow whip, by his side. When I saw the yellow whip, the holy whip for holy student the Dalai Lama, I studied. Out of fear. Even at that age I know, if I study, no holy pain."

The Dalai Lama chuckled at the memory, then he grew serious again. He said, "My approach: Today's reality is whole world just one body. Everything is a part of me. Understanding this helps reduce negative emotions. Hatred comes because we don't appreciate interdependence. Suffering comes because we don't understand interdependence. We cause harm, sometimes unintentionally, because we are greedy for money, power. We think these things will make us happy. This is misunderstanding. Real happiness comes from peace of mind. The only way to obtain is be altruistic, be compassionate."

For the Dalai Lama, the essence of the Buddhist worldview can be summed up in two words: nonviolence and interdependence. Nonviolence for him is not passivity; the absence of violence is only part of it. We need to actively help others and we should do that with a genuine sense of compassion, not pity. At a minimum, we should not harm others. Not harming others is a logical extension of the idea of interdependence. Since everything is a part of us, harming others would hurt ourselves.

One of my all-time favorite commentaries on the subject of interdependence is the following:

A human being is part of the whole, called by us "Universe," a part limited in time and space. He experiences himself, his thoughts and feelings, as something separated from the rest—a kind of optical delusion of his consciousness. This delusion is a kind of prison, restricting us to our personal desires and to affection for a few persons nearest to us. Our task must be to free ourselves from this prison by widening our circle of compassion to embrace all living creatures and the whole of nature in its beauty.

You might think that these words came from the Dalai Lama. And you would be wrong. Einstein wrote them in 1954.

∾

"So, taking care of other," the Dalai Lama told us in Delhi, "taking care of other part of the world, is actually taking care of yourself. Because individual future depends on the humanity as a whole. So that's new reality—global economy and also population and technology and also the environment. So long as you have the feeling, you have the sense of concern about the well-being of others, then there is no room to cheat, no room to exploit, no room to bully. All is part of you, all part of me.

"And it's very important to make distinction: actor and action. We have to oppose bad action. But that does not mean we against that person, actor. Once action stopped, different action comes, then that person could be friend. That's why, today, China is enemy; the next day, there's always the possibility to become friend. And that's why I have no problem forgiving the Chinese for what they've done to my country and people."

THE LITTLE
BEGGAR GIRL

B unker Roy's Barefoot College in Tilonia, India, trained 140 illiterate grandmothers from Africa to be solar engineers in a span of five years. After six months of training, these women would have learned how to assemble and maintain a solar-powered lighting system capable of generating up to five hundred kilowatts per day. By the time they finished the program, they could also put together simple solar lanterns, parabolic solar cookers, and solar water heaters. These grandmothers learned all this by means of sign language and color codes, because of the language barrier. When they left Tilonia and went back to Africa, they were fully capable of electrifying entire villages. The result? Ten thousand homes in twenty-one African countries now have solar power.

Roy, with a touch of his trademark flamboyance, has proclaimed, "Never in the history of Africa have so many women traveled so far away, for so long, to be trained as solar engineers, without knowing how to read, write, or speak the language."

Over the years, I have spent time with Roy in various places in Europe and Asia. He has a finely honed sense of humor and an unassuming way of being. He has an acute sense of his remarkable accomplishments and yet he makes great effort not to take himself seriously. When I first asked him over coffee in Oxford, England, to come to the Delhi gathering in January 2011, he refused outright. He was put off by some of the boldface names. Roy was skeptical that something meaningful would come out of the dialogue. Some months later, when I was able to spend a few days with him in Gangtok, Sikkim, he finally relented. His work helping the poor resonated with the raison d'être of the meeting, and the opportunity to again spend some time with the Dalai Lama clinched the deal.

Inside the Taj Palace Hotel, Delhi, I arranged for Roy to have an on-stage chat with the Dalai Lama immediately after the lunch break. I introduced him and his Barefoot College to the participants and then handed over the microphone.

"Your Holiness," Roy addressed the Dalai Lama, "you might remember when we met in June 2010, in Dharamsala. I took two Tibetan grandmothers along. You said you don't believe these elderly women can be solar engineers. You said too difficult, not possible. And then five months later you met them again in Delhi. They explained to you how they are going to solar-electrify villages near Dharamsala. You were so pleased I could see your eyes light up."

The Dalai Lama nodded. As he listened, he reached inside the folds of his robes, took out a Kleenex, and wiped his nose. He carefully folded the tissue into a neat square and then secreted it back inside his garment.

"Today's meeting here has been extraordinary," Roy continued. "It is wonderful to have so many accomplished humanitarians in one place. Some of us had already started to collaborate, to create programs that would impact the poorest of the poor. We don't need a lot of money to make a difference. But we need our hearts to be in the right place. If our hearts are in the right place, miracles can happen. We talked about magic this morning. This is one miracle we'd like to create with you. Small effort, small actions. They say in Africa that if you don't know what a big difference a small act can make, then you have never been bitten by a mosquito. We need your blessing."

"Certainly, certainly, very good," the Dalai Lama said without hesitation. "This work you are all doing here I consider compassion translated into action. So wonderful. These organizations here, these individuals with lots of experience in the field. So very practical. We have worldwide problems, big gaps between rich and poor people, so we need combined effort. So today's meeting, very useful, should continue from time to time."

A slight smile appeared on the Dalai Lama's face. He cupped a hand behind his right ear and said impishly, "But sometimes when I listen to presentations from people from different fields, their way of talking is almost always: their work is best in whole world. That I don't believe."

He wagged and pointed a finger at Roy: "Including this person also." He bent toward the Indian and proceeded to smack him on the knee with his right hand. Roy grabbed the hand and intercepted the blow. The Dalai Lama extricated his hand and, in an instant, slapped Roy's hand hard. Both men, and everyone in the room, laughed uproariously.

Then the Dalai Lama turned serious. "So we need all experts, more exchange, learning from each other. One great thing about Buddhist teaching is everybody has Buddha nature. That provides us with enthusiasm, self-confidence. If we make effort we can become a Buddha. Buddha never say, 'Oh, I am something special and you must follow my teachings.' Not that way."

I could see that the Dalai Lama was in his element. He was energized by his exchange with Roy. His voice had risen and there was pure conviction on his face. His words came out in short, powerful bursts. "When we deal with poorer people, we should keep that idea. Respect them. We have same potential. Encourage them, praise them sometime. In some human qualities," he continued, "these poorer people more honest, less jealousy. Those big people in big city maybe more jealousy, more suspicion, more worry. So there are reasons to praise the poor. We can learn from them."

Roy extended an arm toward the Dalai Lama respectfully. The lapel mike had fallen loose among the folds of his robe. The Dalai Lama retrieved it and tried to reattach it before continuing: "These people should not feel nobody taking care. We are part of them and they are part of us. Must share together."

"We will promise to share some successful failures," Roy said in his resonant baritone, "to show that we are human. We are not all Superman. We also have doubts, we also have fear just like everybody else. So we will share some failures with you."

The Dalai Lama stopped fiddling with his mike and pointed a finger at Roy. "Recently we were in Gangtok." He was having trouble getting his words out, he was giggling so hard. "I just tease him, his Barefoot College, can it produce nuclear physicists? He said no."

"That's true," Roy said.

"World needs this kind of profession, these physicists. So no matter how wonderful his college, difficult to produce." He bent from the waist toward Roy, touched a hand on his forehead and snapped it forward in a salute.

"Among religious believers also," the Dalai Lama continued. "Due to lack of realistic approach, they feel their religion is best. That's not realistic. Each religion has some unique things. For different people, different religions most effective, so for them that religion is best. Cannot say this religion or that religion is best global-level."

Then, all of a sudden, the Dalai Lama became unusually animated. In the past decade I have often seen him excited, energized, and totally engaged. He was excited when he met Aaron Beck, the distinguished psychotherapist, in a Göteborg hotel. It was a meeting of the minds, a conversation between equals exploring the convergence of ancient Buddhist science with modern cognitive behavior therapy. He was energized when he talked to sixteen thousand young students in a Vancouver hockey arena. The tidal wave of youthful enthusiasm moved him and lifted his spirits as no intellectual discourse on abstract issues ever could. But this time, in the small conference room at the Taj Palace, there was a special gleam in the Dalai Lama's eyes. In a nanosecond, he was transformed. His expression became one of pure wonderment. Everyone in the room felt the energy shift.

"Oh, yesterday one small act," he said, pinching his thumb and forefinger together in front of his face. "I really felt very happy," he said, touching his palm to his heart and leaning out of his chair. "That was when I came from the airport to hotel. Lots of cars and at one time cars stop. Meantime, beside the road, one small, I think girl, I think four or five years old . . ." He bent forward in his chair and extended his arm with palm down to show us her height. He glanced over at the water glasses on the low table in front of him. "Carry one glass, begging." The Dalai Lama held an imaginary glass before him, mimicking the act. "One car, just in front of that young girl, stopped. The girl begged. Nothing happened."

He paused and scratched the right side of his face. He has a mild case of eczema and he would scratch an itch on his face or head from time to time, even when he was meditating.

The Dalai Lama said, "In the past, occasionally I have some money in my bag and I give some. But yesterday, nothing. Then I asked my Indian liaison officer, 'You have some money?' He said, 'Yes.' He gave money to the young girl. Then in my bag, I found the chocolate yesterday I got from the airplane." He turned and pointed to Pierre Omidyar, the founder of eBay, who sat beside me. Omidyar had had an audience with the Dalai Lama the day before, in Dharamsala, and they had traveled together to Delhi on his private plane. Omidyar put his palms together and gave a little bow of acknowledgment.

"So I gave the chocolate to that girl. Oh . . . then, on the face of that child . . ." The Dalai Lama's voice was soft and tender. I sensed the sanctity of the moment. There was pure awe on his face. He gently held his palms in front of his face as if he were holding something incredibly fragile and precious.

"After that, her mother, carrying another young child, coming," he continued. "And that young girl, smiling, the face, and showing joyful experience." He was choked up, reliving the moment, his mind's eye taking in again the child beggar's innocent exuberance. He was having trouble finding adequate words to describe the encounter. I felt slightly uncomfortable to be privy to an emotion so raw and so without artifice.

"I really felt, now at least I gave some virtues," the Dalai Lama concluded. "I really enjoy."

There was total silence in the room. Everyone held his or her breath, unwilling to let the magic slip away.

I was reminded that for much of his life, because of his exalted station, the Dalai Lama has lived within a bubble. When he was in his teens, he would often run up to the lofty parapets of the Potala Palace and peer through his beloved telescope at the hustle and bustle of the Tibetan bazaar in Lhasa. How he would envy the men and women on the street—seemingly so carefree and full of laughter, at least from a distance. He felt impotent; he had no way to interact with them. He could not share their joy or their agony or walk among them, although he cared deeply for their welfare. And he could do little to ease the challenges of their lives on an individual level.

There was one thing he could do, however. Every so often, he would catch sight of small herds of yaks as they passed below the palace gates, being led to slaughter. He would almost always send his servants to buy a few yaks. These animals would be taken up to the courtyard of the Potala and, once there, have red ribbons sewn permanently onto one of their ears. They would henceforth never be butchered but would live out their lives within the palace walls. This was one act, one decision he himself could make, that provided the young Dalai Lama with joy and meaning. It was also a traditional Buddhist way of accumulating merit.

The Dalai Lama closed his eyes for a moment and exhaled audibly. Obviously, he had derived similar pleasure from having the opportunity to give a piece of chocolate to the beggar girl. It was a simple gesture, yet powerful in its effect.

Then his right arm shot out, one forefinger pointing at the group. His face was stern as he said with forceful conviction, "So, similarly, you people, from your pocket, give something to those needy people. I really appreciate. That's the ultimate source of your own happiness. Very clear, very clear."

The Dalai Lama leaned back and settled into his armchair. He has told me several times that all of us, without exception, have some selfish streak. We all want happiness for ourselves. No one wakes up in the morning with the hope that he or she should suffer. As long as we have this "selfish" (albeit involuntary) impulse, we might as well be wise about it. The Dalai Lama has no doubt that the most effective and fail-safe method to achieve genuine, sustainable happiness is simply to care for the well-being of others. This is the "wise selfish" that he talks about. His encounter with the little beggar girl was a good example of what he had told me: Caring for others will often result in surprising but tangible rewards.

The Dalai Lama leaned forward in his chair again. "Of course, not give whole money to the poor." He started to laugh, his knees jiggling up and down from the effort. He glanced at Omidyar and continued: "Must keep some money and make more profit, so that you see, funds continuously come." Pierre Omidyar and his wife, Pam, had just joined the Giving Pledge, an initiative begun by Warren Buffett and Bill Gates. To date, some sixty of America's super-rich have signed on to give the majority of their wealth—about $600 billion dollars and counting—to philanthropy.

The Dalai Lama was not finished yet. He was on a roll. The meeting, with its mission of helping the poor, had galvanized him. He had another anecdote for the small group of humanitarians and social activists.

"One time one family from Bombay came to see me," he said. "The lady asked me blessing. I told her, 'I have nothing to bless you, nothing. Source of blessing is your own hand. You are rich, so out of your own profit use some money and give those poor people, for example the street children in Bombay slums. Give them some education, build some education facilities. Help. That's the real source of blessing,' I told her. That's really the best way to get virtue, merit."

ONLY ONE ROCK STAR

B ono, wearing his trademark shades, strode unhurriedly onto the Cape Town cathedral stage, stuffed his hands casually in his trouser pockets, and sang:

. . . I have scaled these city walls . . .
Only to be with you . . .

He sang the first stanza of his song "I Still Haven't Found What I'm Looking For" alone and without accompaniment. Then a group of luminous people sashayed in behind him: full of colors, movement, and energy. A dozen or so members of the famous Soweto Gospel Choir, resplendent in robes of bold colors and impossibly juxtaposed fabrics of Xhosa and Ndebele design, were in perpetual and exquisite motion. Their voices and percussive claps added rich harmonies to Bono's melodic lines. Now a lone drummer joined them, the staccato beats providing an exuberant rhythm to the song.

Directly in front of me, a woman with long black hair stood up and started to dance. Then Archbishop Emeritus Desmond Tutu, in the next row, also stood up. He shuffled out of the pew toward the stage in time with the music. He jiggled his expressive shoulders and pumped his arms enthusiastically. Then he bent his legs deeply and rocked his hips with abandon. For a man who had just turned eighty, he displayed quite a repertoire of slick dance moves. Tutu had a long white scarf wrapped twice around his neck and a long shirt of a sumptuous shade of deep purple. The last time I had seen him, he had snow-white curly hair fringing his mahogany billiard ball of a head. It was all gone now, and his head was oiled and shiny.

The archbishop, South Africa's spiritual conscience, was partying. And an adoring crowd of celebrities and supporters had come to Cape Town's cathedral to help him celebrate his eightieth birthday.

∾

But the festive atmosphere of Tutu's day in the South African sun was overshadowed by controversy and frustration. Earlier in the week, in a press conference, he had gone on a rampage. I had never seen him so enraged. He shouted, jabbed his finger, and spit out his words with venom. He bellowed to the assembled journalists, "I really can't believe this. You have to wake me up and tell me that this is actually happening, that it is actually happening here in South Africa."

The Dalai Lama was supposed to be the guest of honor at

Tutu's birthday. He was also scheduled to deliver the inaugural Desmond Tutu Peace Lecture at the University of the Western Cape in Cape Town. But on the day of the birthday, October 7, 2011, the South African National Congress (ANC) government still had not issued a visa for the Dalai Lama.

"Unbelievable," Tutu thundered, "the discourtesy the ANC has shown to the Dalai Lama. Anywhere in the world, you have trouble finding a venue large enough to accommodate all the people who want to hear from the Dalai Lama. To treat him like this . . . unbelievable.

"Our government is worse than the apartheid government, because at least you were expecting it from them. The world believes we in South Africa will automatically be on the side of the oppressed. And Tibetans are being oppressed. Hey, Mr. Zuma [the president of South Africa], you and your government don't represent me. I'm warning you. I'm warning you, out of love, like I warned the Nationalists. Watch out. Watch out. One day we will start praying for the defeat of the ANC government."

❧

At the cathedral, Bono told the crowd, "I'm here obviously because I'm not radical enough to be denied a visa. It used to be rock stars, not religious leaders, who caused controversy. But now that I think about it, there is only one rock star in this room." He jabbed a finger at Tutu sitting in the front pew. "And he is sitting in front of me."

Tutu and others have accused the South African government of kowtowing to the Chinese. Tutu said, "Clearly, whether they say so or not, they were quite determined that they are not going to do anything that would upset the Chinese." As I followed Tutu and others out of the cathedral, I saw several protesters holding up a large yellow banner printed with the words SA BETRAYED FOR 30 PIECES OF YUAN. WE ARE SORRY HH THE DALAI LAMA. HAPPY BIRTHDAY ARCH.

The Dalai Lama's response to the denial of the visa was as low-key as Tutu's was fiery. "I'm very eager to see you personally," he said in a video message to Tutu. "I'm very looking forward, this one opportunity to meet you. But however, even till last day, no answer from your government. So then I felt, oh, this is clear sign your government feel very inconvenient. So I cancel my visit. I'm quite sad. I very much also hoping to see Nelson Mandela, very old, so now I doubt whether I'll have another occasion to meet him."

On October 8, 2011, one day after Tutu's eightieth birthday, Google took out a full-page ad in *The New York Times*. The entire page was blank except for a tiny classified ad, centered in the middle, that read:

The Dalai Lama, Tibet's exiled spiritual leader, ~~scrapped plans on Tuesday to attend~~ *joined* the 80th birthday celebration of a fellow Nobel laureate, Desmond M. Tutu of South Africa, *via hangout* after the host government did not grant his visa request.

In the ad, the words "scrapped plans on Tuesday to attend" were struck out by pen and replaced by the handwritten word "joined," and "via hangout" was inserted after "South Africa." That's how Google pitched the idea that the Dalai Lama would use Google Hangouts, a new feature of Google+, to celebrate Tutu's birthday by having a video chat with him on the Internet.

The event was broadcast live from the University of the Western Cape, a short distance away from downtown Cape Town. The entire auditorium was filled with people who had bought tickets to the inaugural Desmond Tutu Peace Lecture, which was supposed to have been delivered by the Dalai Lama in person.

Tutu sat on the stage next to an empty chair. The moderator, Professor Judith Mayotte, sat farther to his right. A large screen showed the Dalai Lama sitting in his residence in Dharamsala, a computer in front of him, an altar and *thanka*s (Buddhist religious paintings) behind him.

Tutu started the hourlong conversation by telling the crowd, "The Dalai Lama, in fact, is quite mischievous. Whenever we are together, I have to warn him: Hey, hey, look here, the cameras are on us, you have to try to behave like a holy man. One time we were in a football stadium in Seattle, sixty thousand people were waiting for him, for someone who can't even speak English properly . . . I want to assure you that I'm not jealous. Really. I am not jealous."

On the large screen, I saw that the Dalai Lama was hunched over the computer, staring at the image of Tutu intently.

"You describe me as mischievous," the Dalai Lama said. "I

also describe you as mischievous, Bishop. Logically, two mischievous persons automatically develop special friendship. You are genuine believer. You always carry true message of Jesus Christ. I consider you a man of truth, a man of honesty. Therefore I develop respect, friendship with you."

Mayotte then asked the two religious leaders how wars could be prevented and how a culture of peace could be built.

"It's actually quite straightforward," Tutu said, and cackled. "Let women take over." He did a little jig in his chair as the crowd cheered.

"That is actually seriously meant," he said after the commotion died down. "Biologically, women are meant to be life-givers. They say: I can't carry baby in my womb for nine months and then agree for it to become cannon fodder. Of all God's creatures, men are the most insecure, but we are good actors. I've found it in myself. In the U.S., I get standing ovations when I speak, and I ought to feel good. But I don't until my wife, Leah, says I'm good. Women, because they are compassionate, they can help society survive. I'm willing to be the chaplain to this movement."

"Science now very clear," the Dalai Lama said. "Calm mind good for health. And calm mind's ultimate source is kind heart, compassionate heart. As individuals become healthier, social relation with others also improve. But how to achieve? Bishop Tutu, may I say frankly? You and I, we are religious persons teaching others. That not sufficient. We have to work through education system, from kindergarten to university. Teach warm heart. It is for our own interest, as important as material well-being. As you rightly mentioned, females more compassionate. Now, to have peaceful century we must promote value of compassion. For that female should take more active role."

Tutu leaned toward the moderator and spoke quietly to her. She nodded and he took the mike.

"My dear brother," Tutu said to the Dalai Lama. "I want to ask you something. Do you have an army?"

The Dalai Lama was surprised by the question. The audience gasped audibly. He pondered for a moment and replied, "Spiritual level, yes, I have army. Not weapon, but wisdom"—he pointed to his head—"and compassion."

"I asked this question to find out why the Chinese government fear you," Tutu said.

"Some Chinese officials describe me as a demon, so naturally some fear of demon," the Dalai Lama said. "When I heard this, I feel like laughing, so I said yes . . . I have horns. I think all totalitarian systems hypocritical. Lies are unfortunately part of life. If someone tells truth, then officials feel uncomfortable—1.3 billions Chinese should have right to know the truth. Censorship is immoral. When I meet Chinese friends, I always tell them China has clear potential to take constructive role on planet. But trust and respect from rest of world important. Transparency is essential."

It was a few days after Tutu's birthday celebration, and we were having tea in his office in Milnerton, a suburb of Cape Town.

"Please say to the doctor," Tutu instructed Vivian Ford, his assistant, who had just walked into his spacious office. "Tell him it is an eighty-year-old man asking for a special favor. Tell him my wife Leah's got asthma. It is under control, but she is coughing and wheezing. Very bad. Tell him if he wants to go to heaven, then he will come and see her."

The archbishop was dressed casually in slacks and a bright red long-sleeved shirt, a memento from the White House Inaugural conference of 2009. A travel suitcase rested next to a desk; he was due to fly soon to Finland, to speak at an event commemorating Global Dignity Day. A framed photo of him with President Obama and the First Lady was on the wall behind the desk. Stacks of music CDs and a photo of a middle-aged Leah sat next to the computer.

After Ford had left the room, I asked Tutu, "What are you going to do with the surfboard, your gift from Pam and Pierre Omidyar?" The Omidyars, founders of eBay, had traveled to Cape Town for the birthday party, bringing presents.

"Pam said she is prepared to give me lessons. I'd go to Hawaii to get lessons from her," Tutu replied happily. I mentally made a note to myself to be there to watch the proceedings if that ever came to pass.

I saw that Tutu had a book by the Dalai Lama on his desk, so I asked him about their uncommon bond.

"It is chemistry. Neither of us had expected that we'd hit it off as well as we did. It came as a gift. One thing about him I found striking. His sanctity. He is holy. He told me about his spiritual practice. He goes to bed very early. Why? Because he spends a huge amount of time meditating and praying every morning. I think that is the reason he is so attractive to so many people. It is clearly not what he says. Although . . . yes, there is profundity there. But it is what is underneath. People are aware he is someone special. That he cares, that he is warmhearted. And he lives what he preaches."

❦

The large courtyard between the Dalai Lama's residence and the Namgyal Monastery in Dharamsala was packed. Upward of a thousand Tibetans and a handful of foreigners sat on the ground under the shelter of a gigantic all-weather canopy. Half a dozen men, sporting snow-lion masks fringed with long white manes, and long skirts and traditional felt boots, bowed deeply toward the large metal gates of the residence. Then, like some crazed whirling dervishes deep in trance, they whiplashed their arms and legs in a dizzying dance that was as energetic as it was mesmerizing. From time to time, they yelled "Waa, hah hah hah hah" in unison.

At the conclusion of the welcome dance, the Dalai Lama—holding the hands of both Tutu and Leah, who had traveled to India from South Africa four months after the bishop's eightieth birthday—slowly led a large retinue of security guards and officials to a bank of couches arranged at the entrance of the monastery. The archbishop was dressed formally in an ankle-length purple robe. A large metal cross dangled in front of his chest. For the first time since the two religious icons had met in the United

States in 2008, the Dalai Lama welcomed Tutu to his home in India.

"I want to say a few words in my broken English," the Dalai Lama told Tutu, who immediately covered his eyes with a hand in mock embarrassment. "In human history some exceptional individuals come. They carry certain views, certain ideas, and they share them with many people. Then they disappear. But their spirit remains, century after century. Bishop Tutu, your spirit will remain, at least through this century. That I'm sure. There are lots of conflicts on the planet. But sooner or later these conflicts will resolve itself, I think. But then some kind of negative feeling here"—he placed a hand on his chest—"governments cannot help much. Only spiritual leaders can help remove these negative feelings."

The weather in Dharamsala in February was decidedly chilly, and Tutu, having just arrived from balmy South Africa, was obviously not used to it. The Dalai Lama had wrapped a dark brown pashmina shawl around Tutu's shoulders, and, for good measure, he added another thick white scarf on top of it. The body of the Anglican cleric was submerged under layers of purple, brown, and white. Only his prominent mahogany head was visible.

"Your Holiness, and all of you beautiful, beautiful people here," Tutu said, "thank you. Thank you. Now I can celebrate my eightieth birthday properly."

The Dalai Lama stood up from his couch, bowed at the waist, and applauded the archbishop.

"It's cold, but Leah and I can feel the warmth of your love," Tutu continued. "I've said this to many people: The Dalai Lama is the holiest person I've ever met. I want to say to the Chinese government: He is the most peace-loving person on earth. Please . . . you leaders in Beijing, we beg you, we beg you, allow the Tibetans to have autonomy, the freedom which is guaranteed under your constitution. We beg you. But we also want to remind you that this is a moral universe. There is no way that injustice, suppression, and evil can ever have the last word. One day we will visit the Dalai Lama in Tibet. God hasten the day when we will enter a free Tibet."

Then the world's two most beloved elders, holding hands, headed into the Dalai Lama's residence for an early lunch.

Acknowledgments

While working on *The Wisdom of Compassion*, I have benefited from the wisdom as well as the compassion of countless people, and I'm grateful to have received such an enormous amount of encouragement and support.

I have had the honor of working closely with Geoff Kloske, the publisher of Riverhead Books, and have enjoyed our many meetings and conversations. Geoff took valuable time out to travel to Canada to attend the 2009 Vancouver Peace Summit featuring the Dalai Lama, an event that I helped convene. He critiqued the manuscript brilliantly and has been a true believer in what we are trying to accomplish. Geoff has a wonderful assistant and editor in Laura Perciasepe, who is one of the most welcoming persons I know in New York. Laura's faith in the project has been enthusiastic and indefatigable. Together they nurtured the book, with a great dollop of patience, to fruition. I'm enormously grateful to them. Noah Lukeman is my literary agent for both *The Wisdom of Forgiveness* and *The Wisdom of Compassion*. He has been a good friend and advocate for more than a decade. I've had the help of many friends who read the manuscript (in part or in whole) and who provided valuable comments: Bonnie Richards, my sister; Anna Kaye and Alex Lau; Ross McDonald; Susan Alexander; Peter Wing; Claire Weeks; Carolyn Walker; Ray Rhamey; Pierre Omidyar; Gretchen Clark; Roberto and Cicci Vitali. Daniel Wood, Barbara Pulling, and Laurie Wagner read versions of the manuscript and provided detailed suggestions. They are wonderful mentors, and they have been consistently helpful with my writing through the years. I met Barbara Standley briefly but serendipitously at a Brooklyn writers' festival. As a keen student of Buddhism, she graciously offered her assistance, and I benefited from her long experience as an editor. Merrie-Ellen Wilcox helped with the copyediting.

Several friends are featured in the book: Richard Moore, Florrie Moore, Charles Inness, Matthieu Ricard, Sir Fazle Hasan Abed, Susan Davis, Bunker Roy, Craig Kielburger, Richard Davidson, Aaron Beck, Eckhart Tolle, Sir Ken Robinson, Kim Schonert-Reichl, Paul Ekman, and Archbishop Emeritus Desmond Tutu. They were all generous with their time and allowed me to interview them at length, providing context and depth to several chapters.

I'm grateful for the friendship of the former and current secretaries in the Private Office of the Dalai Lama: Tenzin Geyche Tethong, Chhime Chhoekyapa, and Tenzin Taklha, a paragon of professionalism and goodwill. His Holiness's representatives Lobsang Nyandak Zayul (New York), Thupten Samdup (London), and Tempa Tsering (New Delhi) have been good and reliable friends over the years. Thanks also to Don Eisenberg and Tenzin Choejok, the social media masterminds in the office. I'm particularly indebted to Ngari Rinpoche, His Holiness's brother, and his wife, Rinchen Khando. Over the past decade they have tirelessly provided fine Tibetan meals, wise counsel, and, above all, steadfast friendship. They have taken to heart the Dalai Lama's compassionate worldview and practice it with unwavering diligence in their daily lives.

Samdhong Rinpoche, Lobsang Sangay, former and current Kalon Tripas, provided moral support and encouragement. I'm thankful to Adam Engle and Diego Hangartner of the Mind & Life Institute for friendship and assistance, especially during the annual conferences in Dharamsala. Thanks also to Jetsun Pema, Thupten Jinpa, Geshe Lhakdor, Tashi Wangdi, Tenzin Priyadarshi, Tenzin Namgyal Tethong, Lodi Gyari, Jim Doty, Rajiv Mehrotra, Robert Thurman, and Dr. and Mrs. Tseten Sadutshang, who are all trusted confidants of His Holiness. My family and I are especially grateful for the gracious hospitality extended to us in Leh, Ladakh, by His Holiness's sister Jetsun Pema, who served for more than four decades as president of the Tibet Children's Villages.

In my travels with the Dalai Lama, I have met many remarkable people; their impact has been felt, but their names are too many to mention. I am especially grateful for the friendship of Austin Hearst, Frank Giustra, Christy Louth, Alison Lawton, Eric Nonacs, Mordehai Wosk, John Lefebvre, Tony and Margo Phillips, Harald and Sharlene Ludwig, Shannon Belkin, Lynn

Green, Gordon Richards, Caroline and Jane Blunden, Larry Brilliant, Pam Omidyar, Patty Gift, James Gimian, Hari Varshney, Praveen Varshney, Marc Kielburger, Matt Banwick, Susan Phillips, Neil Ghosh, Abigail Disney, Chantelle Chouinard, George Wong, Maria LeRose, Tim Kerr, Anthony and Marie-Laure Aris, Peggy Dulany, Jon Kabat-Zinn, Adele Diamond, Daniel and Tara Goleman, Dan Siegel, Joan Halifax, Peter and Jennifer Buffett, Matt and Renee Goldman, Stephen Post, Deepak Chopra, Jeffrey Hopkins, Tenzin Khangsar, Juan Martín Lutteral, Agapi Stassinopoulos, Arianna Huffington, Patricia Graham, Tom and Margot Pritzker, Ashley Judd, David Bornstein, Magnus Bartlett, Lorne Mayencourt, Kevin England, Sam Sullivan, Lynn Zanatta, Mairead Maguire, Marjorie Layden, John Helliwell, Jeff Walker, Robert Ho, Mary Gordon, Swanee Hunt, Ann Veneman, Helene Gayle, Molly Melching, and Mpho Tutu. This book has benefited from their influence and goodwill.

I owe special thanks to my fellow trustees at the Dalai Lama Center for Peace and Education: Brenda Eaton, Evan Alderson, Tom Rafael, Jim Hoggan, Martha Piper, Gwyn Morgan, Geoff Plant, Marjorie-Anne Sauder, and Philip Steenkamp. They joined the board because the Dalai Lama's ideals resonated with them, and they have worked to strengthen the Center beyond the call of duty. I'd also like to thank the Center's advisors, supporters volunteers, and staff.

Susanne Martin is my wife, my muse, and my true soul mate. She spent countless hours going through the manuscript, editing, shaping, red-lining. Her impact on the book, levelheaded and wise, is profound and heroic. She read and reworked the drafts so many times that she may be able to recite the book by heart. I'm profoundly grateful that she has selflessly embraced and helped my endeavors for more than two decades. Our daughters, Lina and Kira, unobtrusively provided moral encouragement. In their subtle ways, they are my best cheerleaders. Poodoo the cat, inimitably aloof, soothed me over the course of the writing and occasionally offered welcome distractions.

Meeting His Holiness the Dalai Lama in 1972 radically transformed the trajectory of my life. Because of him, I learned to ask the question "What would the Dalai Lama do?" with increasing frequency and urgency. In the process, my life became immeasurably more meaningful. It is fair to say that this book would never have existed without his friendship and without the precious opportunities extended to me to witness how one person can embody compassion in so consummate a manner.

Victor Chan